Endorsemer

Simple. Biblical. Practical. Humorous. These words describe Mike Minnix's new book *Senior Christians Living Super Lives*. I have seen these chapters work in Mike's life, and if seniors apply these to their own lives, we will soon be on our way to having the churches and world we have wanted for so long!

—Dr. David Mills, Ph.D. Th.M.
Assistant Professor of Evangelism | Associate Dean for Applied Ministry
Roy Fish School of Evangelism & Missions
Southwestern Baptist Theological Seminary

Dr. J. Mike Minnix provides a game-plan for the fourth quarter in *Senior Christians Living Super Lives*. He understands the importance of playing the last two minutes in the game of life with divine purpose. Read this book if you want to make your life count for the glory of God. I highly recommend it!

—Dr. Franklin L. Kirksey, Pastor
First Baptist Church, Spanish Fort, Alabama
Author of the book, "Sound Biblical Preaching: Giving The Bible A Voice"

I am excited about this book two reasons: I love the author; and I love the audience. Read it, be blessed, and pass it on to someone coming behind you.

—Pastor Johnny Hunt
First Baptist Church, Woodstock, Georgia
President, Southern Baptist Convention,
2008-2010

Dedication

To faithful senior adult Christians I have known, and especially to my wife, Jayne, whom I have observed as a sweet super saint for fifty years!

The New King James Version is used for all Bible references in this book.

CONTENTS

Old age is the most unexpected of all things
that can happen to a man.

—Leon Trotsky, *Diary in Exile*

For age is opportunity no less
Than youth itself, though in another dress,
As the evening twilight fades away,
And sky is filled with stars invisible by day.

—Henry Wadsworth Longfellow

Even to your old age, I am He,
And even to gray hairs, I will carry you!
I have made, and I will bear;
Even I will carry, and will deliver you.

—Isaiah 46:4

FOREWORD

There are various reasons why I am excited to be writing the foreword to this book. Two major reasons are because I love the author and I love the audience. I am not sure that I have ever picked a book up before that referenced the senior adult population. When we begin to realize all the baby boomers moving into that generation, we find that it will be the largest this globe has ever known. I have been privileged to speak in some of the largest senior adult conferences hosted in this nation, and this is a statement that I often begin my talks with, "When this generation passes off the landscape of our country, the church of the Lord Jesus will change drastically."

The senior adults are a unique group of people, especially those who came to know the Lord at a young age. God has given them the wisdom that is recorded in James 3:17, "But the wisdom that is from above is first pure, then peaceable, gentle, willing to yield, full of mercy and good fruits, without partiality and without hypocrisy." The Bible has called them to be a generation of mentors. All of us are aware that there is no greater need than making disciples, and discipling others, and the senior adults have so much to offer in mentoring the generations coming behind them. The Apostle Paul, when training Titus to go to the Island of Crete to raise up leaders, majored on the older teaching the younger. Many times, when some seniors are ready to turn the leadership over to a younger generation, there are those who step up to the plate and feel that they have come into their hour and that God will use them in a mighty way. I often challenge the seniors of this generation to live in such a way that their latter days may be their best days.

Proverbs 19:20 reads, "Listen to counsel and receive instruction, that you may be wise in your latter days." Since the Lord is, indeed, giving us greater wisdom in these latter days, it is my prayer that each person who reads this book, whether you are headed into this stage of your life or you have already arrived, I pray that you will make it your prayer that your legacy would be that you were one who made much of Jesus, and that your latter days were your best days.

My wife is a huge NASCAR fan and oftentimes tells me, "Honey, if you can't watch the entire race, just watch the last ten laps." The truth is that you sometimes only need to watch the last lap, but it seems that many NASCAR races are won in that last ten laps. It is amazing how much is determined in the last laps of the last years of our lives. It is my prayer as I head into the senior years that God will use each of us and that we will finish well. David said it well in Psalms 37:25, "I have been young, and now am old; yet I have not seen the righteous forsaken, nor his descendants begging bread."

I have had the privilege of knowing Pastor Mike Minnix for over 35 years. I remember the first time that I heard him back in 1977, and thought, "This man has the touch of God." There was an unusual anointing on his life. He was preaching a revival at Prospect Baptist Church in Gaffney, South Carolina. It is remarkable that after all these years, my heart was that impressed with the preacher and his message. Following his ministry over these many years, I have seen a man of integrity, a man of character, a man who loves his wife, Jayne, and honors my favorite verse in all of the Bible, Proverbs 20:7, "The righteous man walks in his integrity; his children are blessed after him." It blesses me when I watch his son-in-law take up the mantle and become a mighty pastor also.

As I mentioned in the beginning, I am excited about this book and to be able to write this foreword for two reasons: I love the author; and I love the audience. Read it, be blessed, and pass it on to someone coming behind you.

—Pastor Johnny Hunt
First Baptist Church Woodstock, Ga.
Past President of the Southern Baptist
Convention, 2008-2010

PREFACE

I was walking through my home the other day and saw something that frightened me. There was an old man who had somehow gotten into my house. A surge of adrenaline shot through my arteries, and I was just about ready to attack him when I realized that I was looking in the mirror. Does that sound familiar to you? Have you looked in the mirror lately and wondered how in the world you reached this stage in life? I was shocked by how old I looked because I really didn't feel that old. The question I asked myself was, should I act in accordance with how I look or in harmony with how I feel? In the end, what really matters is what God says we are to do at any given point in our lives.

People are preoccupied these days with looking young. Stores, the Internet, and television commercials provide a wide array of products that "guarantee" to make you look and feel younger. There are pills to swallow, creams to apply, and clothes to buy that promise to make you look and feel more youthful. It is apparent from looking around that most of that stuff is not working.

There is no pill or cream that can make you look young, and a face-lift only works for so long. Also, if you decide to wear the kind of clothes that young people are wearing today, your family may decide to put you in a home somewhere. How do you think Grandpa would look in baggy jeans filled with holes and hanging low enough for his underwear to show? Or how about Grandma with her belly button showing and a butterfly tattoo on her chest? These are not pleasant images.

There is nothing wrong with trying to look young, unless we think that appearing younger will make us happier and more fulfilled. I was amused by what a preacher once said to man who asked if it was proper for a woman to wear makeup. The preacher said, "A little paint never hurt an old barn!" I don't think that preacher was very popular with the women in his church. Certainly we should do things that help us look our best and stay in the best health possible as we age, but it is also important to realize that the most important thing we can do is be the senior adult Christians God has called us to be. Certainly there is nothing wrong with improving our appearance, staying in sound physical condition, and even looking as young as our genes will allow; however, it is more important to continue discovering what it means to serve the Lord in our senior years.

We can, indeed, make the senior years the super years of service for our Lord. We can live a meaningful life now and leave behind a legacy that continues to honor Christ long after we are gone! Every Christian will live forever with the Lord; we are, in essence, ageless. But while we are living, we are forming a heritage for those who come behind us—a positive or a negative one, a good or a bad one! Surely we want to live according to God's plan for us and, thereby, to leave a spiritual legacy that honors our Lord and blesses our families.

I have served the Lord as an ordained minister in a portion of the last six decades. Since I am a senior adult and because so many church members in the twenty-first century are senior adults, I feel compelled to share some biblical truths about serving the Lord as we grow older. Senior adults in our churches and communities can either help *drive the work of God* or be a *drag on the work of God*, depending on their commitment to, attitude toward, and heart for the Lord. Since there are more senior adults living now than ever before, we simply must be committed to making a positive difference for the Lord in our homes, communities, and churches. After reading *Senior Christians Living Super Lives*, it is my prayer that you will be better equipped to contribute your best service to the Lord, to live your most exciting days in the Lord, and to leave behind a faithful legacy for the Lord.

Somewhere I heard the story of a boy walking behind his father in a snowstorm. The wind was howling, and the snow was getting deeper. The boy was stepping directly in the footprints left by his dad. The boy called out, "Daddy, be careful, I'm walking in your footsteps!" The goal of this study is to help us grow in our understanding of how to carefully live in these later years of life so that we leave behind a large meaningful footprint for younger Christians to follow.

This book is laid out in six chapters, each one addressing *practical issues* we face as senior adult Christians. This is not a theological book. *Senior Christians Living Super Lives* is designed to deal with down-to-earth issues that all senior adult Christians face as they live and serve the Lord. A lot of the things discussed in this book deal with life within our individual hearts and in our relationships to other Christians, especially those we encounter in the church.

At the end of each chapter, there are questions to help us think through the scriptures we have read and the thoughts we have considered. Taking time to answer the questions will enhance your personal study and will help you apply what you learn or relearn while reading the book. If you are in a group study, some time should be spent discussing how different individuals answered the questions at the end of each chapter; doing this will aid in understanding how we see things differently as we study and will broaden our perspectives through the eyes of others. In the end, the goal is to continue our growth in the Lord and our faithful service for the Lord no matter our age or what milepost we are passing in our journey of faith. Let's study prayerfully and thoughtfully so we can leave some clear godly footprints for those who follow.

INTRODUCTION

In a 2006 *Newsweek* interview, Billy Graham said, "All my life I've been taught how to die, but no one taught me how to grow old."[1] I agree with Dr. Graham; I was never taught how to grow old either. Every person past sixty years of age can likely identify with Graham's statement. And to be sure, there are a lot more of us living longer now than ever before in human history. Some posit that there are more people over sixty years old living on earth today than have ever lived beyond that age in the prior history of mankind. For example, the population in America rose by three hundred percent from the year 1900 to the year 2000. But the population of people over sixty rose by 1,100 percent during that same time; that means that seniors increased almost four times faster than the general population during the last century! In the United States Census of 2000, there were about thirty-five million people over sixty-five living in America. In the census of 2010, there were more than 40 million people sixty-five or older.[2] In other words, the population of senior adults in America grew by approximately fifteen percent in just ten short years. So if you are a senior adult, you are not alone—not by a long shot. You are living in greater numbers than ever before, and this is vitally important for those of us who are Christians, and it has implications for the church moving into the future.

Mickey Mantle, the late great baseball player for the New York Yankees, is purported to have been one of the people who said, "If I knew I was going to live this long, I would have taken better care of myself."[3] When we are young, we have no idea how it feels to be old. In fact, we often think that older people, with the exception perhaps of our grandparents, already have one foot in the grave.

Young people do not know that *human bodies grow old, but human hearts do not.* Some years ago I saw an interesting interview on a television program. I don't remember the channel or program I was watching, but I will never forget what the elderly lady said during that interview. The woman being interviewed was celebrating her one hundredth birthday, and she was asked by a television reporter how it felt to be a hundred. The centenarian lady was sitting in a chair with a shawl over her shoulders, looking every bit the age she had acquired. Her answer to the question the reporter asked was stunning and insightful. She said very slowly, "I feel like a seventeen-year-old girl looking out the through the windows of an old house." Yes, exactly! Age changes our bodies, but our minds and hearts still view the world with wonder.

Age does change us; that cannot be questioned. As we grow older, we tire more easily, remember things more slowly, and can, if we are not careful, view young people as absolutely nuts. It can be hard for us to remember just how absentminded and irresponsible we were at their age. Also, we can begin to feel that we have done all that we need to do and that it is time for us to take it easy. We can take the posture that it is time for people to recognize our advanced age by treating us with extraordinary deference. For the Christian who is a senior, this kind of thinking is unwise, unhealthy, and counterproductive.

As senior adult Christians, we need to consider the incredible contributions we can still make for the kingdom of God on earth. We need to realize the worth we have as servants for the Lord and be reminded of the amazing opportunities that exist for us to honor Him and His cause in significant ways. We need fellowship, good food to share with each other, and time to travel with our Christian friends, but there is much more we can and should do for the Lord in our senior years of life.

The issue of remaining faithful in service applies uniquely to our participation in the local church. It is critical that we stay busy in service for the Lord; otherwise, we can incorrectly conclude that the church is simply here to serve us rather than seeing that our lives inside and outside the church are to be channels of

God's love, power, and grace to others. We must never allow ourselves to think that our days of service are over.

J. B. Priestley wrote, "There was no respect for youth when I was young, and now that I am old, there is no respect for age. I missed it coming and going."[4] Those of us who are senior adults can certainly indentify with that statement. Bette Davis said, "Old age is no place for sissies." Both Priestley and Davis were right. Physical pain, limited agility, diminishing strength, more modest income, and the sorrow of watching family members and friends precede us in death can make the senior years onerous, sad, and lonely. Often our family members are busy with their own lives, and missing the contact with them can add to the sense of seclusion that we feel. But it doesn't have to be that way. We can take steps to improve the quality of these years and use them to increase the significance of our Christian legacy. We can make contact with people rather than wait for them to make contact with us. We can serve others rather than wait for someone to serve us.

Thirty years ago I pastored a church in North Carolina. One lady in the church sent me and my wife a birthday card every year. We were young then, and she seemed sweet but "old" to us. Yet for the past thirty years, she has continued to send us birthday cards. No matter where we lived or moved, she found our address and sent us those sweet encouraging cards. It was her ministry. I can't tell you the times her little notes lifted our spirits in the service of the Lord. She did not sit by and wait for someone to contact her; she stayed in touch with others personally and through her cards and notes. I learned later that she sent cards to many people, often writing cards every day. God bless her, and may her tribe increase!

Remaining engaged in God's work can and will produce a mind-lift and a heart-lift, and they are better than a face-lift any day! This book was written to help you experience a mind-lift and a heart-lift. In this book we are going to learn or remind ourselves of ways to live as *super senior saints* through continuing or developing the right attitudes and actions for greater service to God and others! We will do this by turning to God's Word and studying some people and statements that furnish us with clear lessons for developing six habits that will honor God, help others, and fill these days of our lives with divine blessings. By the time you finish this book, I pray that you are standing on tiptoe, looking forward each new day God gives you in this world and ready for a glorious homecoming in the world to come!

SERVE

JESUS, OUR EXAMPLE

A couple came forward during the invitation to join the local church. The pastor asked what church they were transferring from. The husband hesitated for a moment and then sheepishly replied, "I'm transferring from the city golf course."

Serving the Lord requires that we set our priorities in proper order. It means to put the Lord first, and that will necessarily mean that we must place some other things lower on the list of priorities. Getting involved fully in the service of the Lord means transferring our loyalty from our own interests to His interests. Of course, this doesn't mean that we can't have hobbies and activities to enjoy, but fully serving God does mean that we need to set aside lesser things to do the greater things.

There is no better example of service than that of Jesus. After all, He left heaven to come to this sinful world in order that He might die for our sins! He came to serve, and He calls us to serve. To serve God correctly, we need to follow the model set by our Lord.

On the Thursday night before Jesus was crucified on Sunday, He met with His disciples in the Upper Room. The disciples had arrived at the Upper Room before Jesus, but when our Lord came into the room, He noticed immediately that a common act of courtesy had been omitted. In those days, when people gathered for a meal, a servant would greet the guests and gently wash their feet. The roads and paths were dusty, and the sandals most people wore provided little protection for the feet against the dirt and dust. Washing the feet was an act of kindness and made any social gathering, especially one involving food, more comfortable and tidy for everyone involved.

Observing that no disciple had taken on the task of washing the feet of the others, Jesus took a basin of water and a towel and began to wash the feet of His disciples. It was, without doubt, an awkward moment for the disciples; after all, this was something one of them should have done for the others before Jesus arrived. Sadly, not one of the disciples had been willing to reduce himself to being a servant to the group. Apparently, each was too proud to bow before the others to wash their feet. Jesus, however, took on the responsibility and accepted the undignified place of service among those men.

Once Jesus had accomplished the menial chore of foot washing, He reminded them of something that all of us as followers of Christ must learn and relearn.

> So when He had washed their feet, taken His garments, and sat down again, He said to them, Do you know what I have done to you? You call Me Teacher and Lord, and you say well, for so I am. If I then, your Lord and Teacher, have washed your feet, you also ought to wash one another's feet. For I have given you an example, that you should do as I have done to you. Most assuredly, I say to you, a servant is not greater than his master; nor is he who is sent greater than he who sent him. If you know these things, blessed are you if you do them.

John 13:12–17

A call to follow Jesus is a call to be a servant. The word 'servant' used by Jesus is a word that speaks of voluntary submission in service to another. Jesus set the example for service by voluntarily washing His disciple's feet. He did not do this to set forth an ordinance for observance in a church worship service; rather, He set forth an example for how we are to act in service to Him and to others. We are to serve and not to wait for others to serve us. If our Lord, who was and is the King of glory, could bow down to serve sinful men, how much more should we serve each other? In fact, Jesus told us clearly that a servant is not greater than His master; since He is our Master, we must humbly serve as He served.

Think carefully about what Jesus did. Though Jesus knew that just a few hours later He would be arrested in the Garden of Gethsemane and that the next day He would die on the Cross, He took the time to serve others. You and I must avoid reaching the point in our Christian lives that we crave being served by others. Our last years can be, and should be, our best years of service. We should do this because it is exactly what Jesus did and what He taught every true disciple to do; however, serving has a positive effect upon the one who serves as well. When you, as a senior adult Christian, serve others, it helps keep you younger, happier, and healthier than being served.

It is crucial that you understand what Jesus was going through the night He washed the disciples' feet. He was experiencing an agony that we cannot imagine. The awful reality of the coming crucifixion was steadfastly in His mind. His willingness to serve His disciples, even during a time of personal anguish, reveals the depth of love and devotion He had for us. Though we can never serve to the extent He did, we can emulate Him. The scripture teaches that this is exactly what we are supposed to do. We must be willing to serve even when we are going through our own trials and difficulties. If we wait till everything is perfect in our lives before deciding to serve, we will never get around to doing God's work.

In Mark 10:45, Jesus said, "For even the Son of Man did not come to be served, but to serve, and to give his life as a ransom for many." Jesus said this when speaking to His disciples about the difference in the way the people of the world view life and the way He wanted them to view and live life. He told them that anyone who desired to be great among them had to do so by being a servant. This is totally contrary to the way the world views greatness. We are not better than our Master, so it is incumbent upon those of us who call Him Lord to serve Him and others voluntarily, lovingly and faithfully.

LORDSHIP DEMANDS SERVICE

When Jesus instructed the disciples in John 13:12–17 concerning the issue of service, He did so in a very revealing way. Jesus said, "You call me teacher and Lord, and you do well." But then Jesus turned the entire statement around and said, "If I then, your Lord and Teacher, have washed your feet, you also ought to wash one another's feet." Note the change in the order of the words that Jesus used. The disciples had put the title teacher before the title Lord. Jesus spoke of the title Lord before He spoke of Himself as teacher. There is a distinctive difference in the order of the words the disciples used and the order of the words Jesus used. He was revealing to all of us that viewing Him first and foremost as Lord will always lead us to greater acts of humble service. Indeed, Jesus is Lord, and when we treat Him as such, we will enthusiastically serve Him and others with an attitude of humility and gratitude. We will have far less concern about our status among our peers and far more interest in emulating the servant-life of our Lord.

Why did the disciples refuse or neglect to take on the task of washing each other's feet? The problem for the disciples in the Upper Room was likely one of pride. Of course, part of it could have been laziness. Indeed, it could also have been a sense of entitlement. Whatever the reason, it was not in keeping with the attitude and teaching of Christ. I suspect that the disciples felt ashamed when Jesus bowed down before each one of them to wash their feet. The moment was definitely an uncomfortable one for each of them. I wonder if we would feel that same sense of embarrassment if Jesus entered our churches or homes and took on the least position of service among us and, thereby, revealed how arrogant so many of us can be at times? Just ask yourself, when was the last time you took on the dirtiest, lowest, and least task of service to others without ever drawing attention to it?

In matters of service, as senior adult Christians, we must be careful not become proud or lazy. Certainly, we have more experience than younger Christians and we tire more easily as well, but that does not provide us with an excuse for failing in the area of service, and it does not offer us justification for thinking our way is always the right way. Submitting to Jesus in matters of service will make us humble, sweet, and gentle in our attitudes and actions.

Of course, the foot-washing experience in the Upper Room took on new meaning to the disciples the next day for that was the day Jesus bore His cross up the hill outside Jerusalem to die for the sins of the world. No act of service could have been more humiliating or painful than the act of service that Jesus took upon Himself when He bore our transgressions at Calvary and accepted the stripes that our sins deserved. If you and I keep the cross of Calvary in our hearts and minds, we will never see a task of service as being too lowly or inconsequential for us to perform for our Lord, and we will never view ourselves as being too important to bow humbly in submissive service to Him and to others.

SERVE THE LEAST OF THESE

A number of years ago, my wife Jayne and our son Chris encountered a woman who was, by all appearances, very poor. Jayne was asked if she would drive the lady to a place where she might apply for some financial assistance. The woman's body gave off an odor so strong that it was all Jayne could do to endure it without becoming sick to her stomach. Jayne agreed to drive the lady to the appointed location, but by the time Jayne and Chris, our son, got back to our home, they were both nauseated by the smell that was left in the car. It was so bad that she had to leave the car doors open for several hours for either of us to endure driving the car at all. What my wife had done was not just help a poor lady; she had served Jesus. Serving Christ is not always comfortable, but it is always the right thing to do. The odor of service for Jesus may not be pleasant to us, but it emits a pleasant fragrance to the Lord when He observes it! Listen to what Jesus said:

> When the Son of Man comes in His glory, and all the holy angels with Him, then He will sit on the throne of His glory. All the nations will be gathered before Him, and He will separate them one from another, as a shepherd divides

31

his sheep from the goats. And He will set the sheep on His right hand, but the goats on the left. Then the King will say to those on His right hand, "Come, you blessed of My Father, inherit the kingdom prepared for you from the foundation of the world: for I was hungry and you gave Me food; I was thirsty and you gave Me drink; I was a stranger and you took Me in; I *was* naked and you clothed Me; I was sick and you visited Me; I was in prison and you came to Me."

Then the righteous will answer Him, saying, "Lord, when did we see You hungry and feed *You,* or thirsty and give *You* drink? When did we see You a stranger and take *You* in, or naked and clothe *You?* Or when did we see You sick, or in prison, and come to You?" And the King will answer and say to them, "Assuredly, I say to you, inasmuch as you did *it* to one of the least of these My brethren, you did *it* to Me."

Then He will also say to those on the left hand, "Depart from Me, you cursed, into the everlasting fire prepared for the devil and his angels: for I was hungry and you gave Me no food; I was thirsty and you gave Me no drink; I was a stranger and you did not take Me in, naked and you did not clothe Me, sick and in prison and you did not visit Me."

Then they also will answer Him, saying, "Lord, when did we see You hungry or thirsty or a stranger or naked or sick or in prison, and did not minister to You?"Then He will answer them, saying, "Assuredly, I say to you, inasmuch as you did not do *it* to one of the least of these, you did not do *it* to Me." And these will go away into everlasting punishment, but the righteous into eternal life.

Matthew 25:31–46

We must look at opportunities for service as occasions to honor Jesus and serve Him. Service does not mean taking the most important and prominent places, nor is it making sure everyone knows what we have done. The Lord knows how, when, and why we served, and that is all that matters. The passage from Matthew 25 points out an interesting truth. On the Day of Judgment, some people will be recognized for acts of service that no one really noticed as important. In fact, at the Judgment, the Lord will identify acts of service done in His name that even the people who performed them did not recognize as all that significant. Others who thought their works were worthy of attention will discover that their acts of service lacked humility and were aimed at getting attention or getting ahead. There will be some surprises on that day! We must always serve with the right motive, and that motive is to reflect the love of Jesus.

A church I pastored a few years ago was in the process of building a new building, and a faithful church member called to tell me to go by his home and pick up a check as a contribution toward the building expense. I drove by his home, and his wife handed me a check for $500,000. It was given without fanfare of any kind. The family that gave this gift never asked that anyone be told about it; rather, they did not want their name announced in regard to this sacrificial gift. Another church member called and said that he would like to help out with some of the labor to save the church money in the building process. He talked to me privately about his desire to help; he did not announce it in a worship service. One family had the means to give a large sum of money, and they did so. Another family had little money to give, but they could provide labor. Each gave what each had! Neither of these families sought any attention for their efforts. In God's eyes, it is likely their gifts were equal! This is what you and I must do if we are to be found faithful in the service of our Lord. We must not consider any requirement that Jesus places before us as being too great or too small. *Each must do what each can with what each has!*

As senior adults, we must be careful not to expect others to serve us; we must serve Christ by serving in whatever ways we can. We must do what we can do with what we have at the time. Some refuse to serve because they feel their contribution will be too small to have an impact. We need to be aware that no service done with loving commitment to Christ is too small.

- The small lunch provided by a little boy fed five thousand people once it was in the hands of Jesus.

- Moses had a wooden staff in his hand, but once dedicated to God, it revealed a faith in God that opened the Rea Sea and provided a path of safety to God's people.

- David had a small sling and five smooth stones, but committed to the Lord, that sling and just one stone brought down the vile giant Goliath.

Do what you can with what you have, and trust God to bless it for His own purposes.

> If you can't preach like Peter,
> If you can't pray like Paul,
> Just tell the love of Jesus,
> And say He died for all.[5]

An older husband and wife joined a church I was pastoring early in the 1990s. They were a sweet Christian couple with a deep devotion to Christ. They have moved to the Atlanta, Georgia area to be near family in their later years. The wife experienced a broken hip and had surgery to have it replaced. She then went to a rehab center for a couple of weeks to improve her motion and agility. I visited her at the hospital and the rehab center. I could tell that the rehab process was not comfortable or easy for her. Once while visiting, I said, "I'm sorry this happened to you and that you are going through this painful process." She smiled and said, "Oh, no, pastor don't say that. I am in the right place for the Lord to use me. You see, I have been witnessing to the nurses here and yesterday I led one of them to the Lord. I have prayed with a couple of others who are going through tough marriages or other problems. I am not excited that my hip was broken, but if this had not happened, I never would have been able to share with these ladies about the Lord and His Word."

Needless to say, I came away from that visit with tears in my eyes. So many people who go through problems ask their minister, "Why am I going through this situation?" But this lady was rejoicing in her troubles because it had given her the opportunity to share her faith and to serve Jesus in a more fruitful way. As I left the rehab center that day, I asked God to help me as a middle aged pastor to never forget that story and to do all I could to emulate that dear Christian lady as I grew older. Again, we each must do what we can, with what we have, where we are!

CALEB, AN INSPIRATION IN SERVICE

Caleb is a man who lived wholeheartedly for the Lord, and he left a great legacy by doing so. I call him a super senior saint. When the Hebrew people were delivered from slavery to the Egyptians, they began a journey toward the Promised Land—Canaan. After some weeks of traveling across the desert, they came to the border of the land God had promised them. Twelve spies were chosen to search out the land and bring back a report; one of those spies was a man named Caleb. Ten of the spies gave a fearful report describing the terror of the giants they had encountered there. Joshua and Caleb reminded the people of God's promise to give them the land and reminded them that it was a land filled with milk and honey. In the end, the people believed the report of the ten negative spies, and thus they did not want to risk entering Canaan. Sadly, all the adults among the Hebrews were condemned to spend forty years wandering in the wilderness till they died, and only Joshua, Caleb, and the descendants of the faithless people were allowed to enter the land after those forty years had passed.

Caleb was one of the faithful spies who tried to get the people to go forward into Canaan. When Caleb had originally gone to spy out the land, he was given a promise from the Lord that he could have a particular mountainous area in the Promised Land as his very own. For forty years, Caleb was forced to wander around in the desert because the majority of the Hebrews had been unwilling to trust God and do God's will, but Caleb never lost faith in God's promise nor did he lose his temper with the doubting crowd of Hebrews.

After forty years of meandering in the desert, the last of the doubters had died, and Joshua finally led the people over the Jordan River and into the Promised Land. Once they arrived in the Promised Land, Caleb asked for the mountain he had been promised. In did not matter to Caleb that giants still occupied that mountain, nor did it matter to him that he had grown much older, reaching the ripe old age of eighty-five. Neither the presence of giants nor the passage of time had dissuaded Caleb from the faith and courage to take the mountain he had been promised. Caleb was committed to the Lord and to the promises of the Lord. He would not sell out, not even in his senior years.

STANDING UP AND NOT SELLING OUT!

I heard about a preacher who was asked by a man to perform his brother's funeral. Neither of the men had been churchgoers or had shown any religious inclinations. The man offered to give $100,000 to the church if the preacher would call his deceased unrighteous brother a saint during the funeral. The preacher knew that the deceased brother had been a regular scallywag all his life, and this presented a problem for the pastor. He knew the church needed the money for the building, but he also knew that everyone who attended the funeral would know that the deceased man was far from a saint. What was the pastor to do? The preacher's assistant asked, "You're not going to do it, are you?"

The pastor said that he was going to do it because the church needed the money. The word got out that the preacher had sold out to the family for money, and the church was filled with people ready to hear the pastor call the sinful, wicked, deceased man a saint. The preacher stood up before the crowded congregation, and this is what he said, "The man we are burying here today was a liar, a cheat, and a drunk. However, next to his brother who is sitting here on the front row, he was a saint!"

WHOLEHEARTED SERVICE

I'm not sure whether the pastor got the promised $100,000, but he did not sell out to the world or for money! We must never sell out to this world or what it has to offer us. Caleb was a man who was firm in his faith and was committed to the Lord all the way to the end. Caleb was so committed to the Lord that the Scripture tells us several times that he was a man who *wholeheartedly* served the Lord. He kept his enthusiasm during all those years of wandering through the wilderness. Nothing had deterred him from God's promised goal. Nothing had diminished his hopes and dreams.

As senior adult believers, we must keep our commitment to the Lord through every circumstance. Serving the Lord calls for a faith that does not wane with time and a commitment does not diminish even if others are not following the Lord faithfully. Caleb kept his faith though the fear and disobedience of others had caused the entire nation to meander in the desert for forty years.

How can we be inspired by Caleb's example? Most of us become discouraged when we see others unwilling to help with a cause. We can give up simply because we feel that we are serving alone. In fact, when you serve the Lord, people will often complain about the service you provide. Circumstances like these make it difficult to maintain a heart of service, but we must not allow lazy people and naysayers to hinder our faithful service for God. Caleb never became disheartened even though thousands of his fellow Hebrews lacked faith to believe God's promise. There is not one verse that displays Caleb as ever being bitter, angry, or unenthusiastic about reaching the Promised Land and the mountain God had promised him.

Let's look at some factors that made a difference in Caleb's attitude and his actions.

WE MUST COMMUNICATE WITH GOD

First, we need to stay in *communication with God*. In Joshua 14:6, we see these words:

What the Lord said...

Caleb remembered what the Lord had said to him. He did not base his faith or service on circumstances but on God's promises. Numerous preachers through the years have expressed this by saying, "God never told us to sit on the premises. He told us to stand on the promises!" Caleb was standing on the promise God had given him, and nothing could discourage him.

In Numbers 14:24, we read how God promised Caleb a mountainous piece of land in Canaan after Caleb had served as one of the faithful spies. That happened when Caleb was about forty-five years old. The land promised to Caleb was Hebron, the hill country south of Jerusalem. So Caleb set his goals according to God's plan for his life and lived every day with God's Word and promise in his heart.

Determination is required in order to live each day according to God's plan for us. God's plan will not always lead us down a smooth path; His plan sometimes leads uphill and against the wind for long periods. But God's plan is always the right one for our lives. This means that we must be willing to serve Him faithfully no matter what the conditions or situations we encounter in life. We must do this no matter how others are acting or failing to act. Caleb did not become dispirited even though others simply could not or would not see a vision for victory in the Promised Land.

WE MUST HAVE A CONVICTION ABOUT GOD

Secondly, we must have a firm *conviction about God*. God expects us to be faithful under all conditions. Caleb did not whine or complain that he had lost forty years due to the negligence of faithless people in his generation. He did not look for an excuse or reason to forget the mountain that God had promised him. He did not use his advanced age as a reason to sit down and give up his original goal. Caleb believed that God was providing him with strength and power to overwhelm the enemies at Hebron. It wasn't that Caleb was confident about his own ability, but that he had full faith and confidence in God's ability to keep His Word and fulfill His promise.

Caleb's conviction about God's promise did not make him arrogant or hateful. There is no record that Caleb spent time grumbling about the faithless people who caused the forty wasted years in the wilderness. It would have been easy for Caleb to become bitter and to have shown animosity and resentment in his attitude and words, but he kept his eyes on the Lord and his faith fixed on God's promise to him.

A conviction about God's will for our lives must never cause us to become self-aggrandizing or haughty in our attitude or speech. Like Caleb, we must hold on to our faith while acting toward others with love and consideration. In fact, there is no account in the scriptures of Caleb ever saying "I told you so" to those who had caused the entire nation to wander around in a desolate land for forty years. Caleb never acted high and mighty when his faith in God's promise proved to be correct. When we are right and others are wrong, we are still required to be gentle and considerate. Even when we know we are right about something and we know that others are wrong about it, we must maintain a humble and loving spirit!

WE MUST MAINTAIN OUR COMMITMENT TO GOD

Thirdly, we must make a *commitment to God* and keep it!

The Bible tells us that Caleb "followed the Lord wholeheartedly."

David wrote in Psalm 16:8, "I have set the Lord always before me."

Paul said in Philippians 3:13, "One thing I do."

We must keep our commitment strong in all situations and under all conditions. That is what Caleb did.

> My heart to love Him,
> My will to obey Him,
> My mind to think on Him,
> My feet to follow Him,
> My tongue to praise Him,
> My knees to bow to Him,
> My lips to witness for Him![6]

Commitment is never dependent on what someone else does; it is always contingent upon our own devotion to the Lord. Caleb was not worried about what anyone else did, said, or thought; he only wanted to please God. After all, if you please God, it doesn't matter who you displease. If you displease God, it doesn't matter who you please. What God thinks about any situation is the important issue, and how we respond to Him is the key to victory or the path to defeat. True success means to press on toward the goals God has for us, and that is only possible when we move in the direction of God's vision for our lives. When we do this, God places His stamp of approval on our lives. Victory only occurs when we have an all-out commitment to Him. Serve the Lord as an act of total commitment.

WE WILL CONQUER THROUGH GOD
Fourthly, we can *conquer through God.*

If we listen to God, have complete conviction about His promises, and then make a commitment to serve with a positive and faithful spirit, we will be victorious! Caleb did defeat the giants and conquer the mountain at Hebron. At eighty-five years of age, he did what many thirty-year-old people would never have attempted.

MARCHING TO ZION
We are not tiptoeing through the tulips in the Christian life; we are marching to Zion! *Our life for Christ is not meant to be a picnic but a spiritual battle.*

> Finally, my brethren, be strong in the Lord and in the power of His might. Put on the whole armor of God, that you may be able to stand against the wiles of the devil. For we do not wrestle against flesh and blood, but against principalities, against powers, against the rulers of the darkness of this age, against spiritual hosts of wickedness in the heavenly places. Therefore take up the whole armor of God, that you may be able to withstand in the evil day, and having done all, to stand.

43

> Stand therefore, having girded your waist with truth, having put on the breastplate of righteousness, and having shod your feet with the preparation of the gospel of peace; above all, taking the shield of faith with which you will be able to quench all the fiery darts of the wicked one. And take the helmet of salvation, and the sword of the Spirit, which is the word of God; praying always with all prayer and supplication in the Spirit, being watchful to this end with all perseverance and supplication for all the saints.
>
> Ephesians 6:10–18

We cannot read these verses properly without comprehending that we are called to be faithful to Christ even as a soldier is to be faithful to his commander. This requires preparing ourselves mentally, morally, ethically, and most importantly, spiritually, so that we can be disciplined in our walk with God.

Paul wrote to Timothy in 2 Timothy 2:3, "You therefore must endure hardship as a good soldier of Jesus Christ." Serving the Lord is not easy nor is it meant to be. We are like soldiers in an army. In God's Christian army, we are not battling against flesh and blood but against a dark, evil enemy in the spiritual realms.

In the 1960s I was in the US Army, and during that time I served a tour of duty in Vietnam. I can assure you that our goal as soldiers was considered a serious duty. We were in a war zone, and people were being wounded or dying every day. As Christians, we must consider our lives as a serious effort to live honorably for Christ in a "spiritual war zone." People are dying without Jesus every day. Christians are hurting and need our prayers and love. We must never take our duty to the Lord lightly. Age does not exempt us from being faithful to Christ.

THIS IS SERIOUS BUSINESS

There is a story of a man way back in the country who wanted to buy some life insurance. He called the insurance man, who promptly came out to the country home to sell the man a life insurance policy. The agent said, "Now, I will need to get some information about your family and health information concerning your parents in order to work out a policy and premium."

The country bumpkin said, "Well, my daddy died a few years ago." The agent asked what killed him. The country man spoke with a Southern drawl and said, "I don't know what killed him, but it weren't nuthing serious." Well, I expect the man who died considered it serious!

We can only drive out the giants with total faithfulness to God and with the realization that this is serious business. We require God's power to overcome the enemy. Listening to Him, believing in Him, and being committed to Him is the only way to have any chance of overcoming the sin-giants of frustration, laziness, indifference, faithlessness, envy, jealousy, and all the other things that can keep us from victory.

Caleb conquered the hill country, the mountainous area called Hebron, through communication with God, confidence in God, and commitment to God. Interestingly, *Hebron* comes from a Hebrew word meaning "fellowship." Caleb did not want the hill country as a selfish position, but rather he desired it in order that he might have a place of fellowship with God and fellowship with God's people. He did not want the seaside country of ease. He did not want the Valley of Eschol, which represented pleasure and satisfaction in the flesh. He did not want Moriah, which represented pride and a human position of prominence. He wanted Hebron, which meant fellowship with God and fellowship with God's people, and which also represented a tremendous defeat for the enemy.

How many of us really want to take on the tasks that require the most from us? To defeat the enemy and bring glory to God, we must be willing to take on the most difficult responsibilities. That is what Caleb wanted, and that is what he obtained! *Sadly, many Christians are living on molehills instead of dwelling on mountaintops.* As a senior adult Christian, you will discover new joy and strength when you are willing to take the high ground! Taking the high ground requires a deep commitment to serving the Lord and others.

LIVING THE LEGACY!

It is important to note that Caleb also became a blessing to others. If you read the full story of Caleb's victory, you will see that he passed on the property at Hebron to his daughter and son-in-law. He was, in fact, a channel of God's blessings to others. He left behind a legacy to his family and to his nation that serving God is worthwhile. That is really what service is about. Too many Christians look at the Christian life and ask "What is in it for me?" To live victoriously, seek ways to honor God and ways to bless those who are coming behind you.

During a church business meeting in the 1970s, a young businessman stood to oppose erecting a new building in our church. The church was growing rapidly, and there were no rooms available for the children and adults who were attending weekly Bible study. After the young man sat down, I recognized a white-haired senior adult lady who wished to speak concerning the proposed building. She said, "The sanctuary you are worshipping in today was built during the Great Depression. Most of us worked in the cotton mills around here, and we had very little money. Some of us ladies decided to give up the one luxury we enjoyed—a five-cent soft drink we had once a day during break at the mill. We took those nickels and brought them to the church to help pay for this sanctuary. We made quilts with leftover cloth at home and sold them around town and gave all the money to the church. Today, most people drive to the church in nice cars and wear beautiful clothes. You eat out and enjoy many advantages we didn't have. If you can't build this building now with all you have to enjoy in life, it will never be built." When we took the vote for the new building, even the man who stood to speak against it voted for it! One dear, precious, committed senior adult lady carried the day. She had been through the wilderness, and God had given her victory. She was not about to doubt that the Lord would do it again, and she intended to urge younger Christians to trust the Lord!

When I am old, how glad I will be,
If the light of my life has been burned up for
thee.
I shall be glad whatever I gave,
Of Labor, or money, one soul to save.
I shall not mind that the way has been rough,
That thy dear feet led the way is enough.
When I am dying, how glad I shall be
If the light of my life has been burned up for
thee!

Imagine if Caleb lived today. He might come to church angry because the building is too cold or too hot for his convenience, or perhaps he would complain because someone is sitting in his favorite seat. Then again, he might threaten not to attend anymore because they no longer sing his beloved hymns.

Actually, the type of man that Caleb was would not have allowed himself to get caught up in petty issues of personal preference. We need an army of Calebs in our churches today. God used Caleb, even in his old age, because Caleb was willing to believe God and act on that belief. The Bible is replete with the stories of people who overcame obstacles in order to serve God and leave a legacy of faithfulness:

- Moses–the tongue-tied shepherd stood up to the pharaoh and won!
- Gideon–the least of his tribe was supported by an army of three hundred armed only with

trumpets, lamps and jars; they fought the Midianites and won!

- David–untrained and unprotected, he challenged Goliath and won!
- Caleb–eighty-five years old, confronted the giants in Hebron and won!
- the early disciples–set out to conquer the Roman world with nothing but the Gospel, and they won!
- Jesus–on the cross He looked like history's greatest loser, but He stood up to Satan and revealed Himself the greatest winner of all time on resurrection morning!

How did all of these people, whom the world most certainly considered losers at the time, turn out to be winners? It was because the power of God flowed through their lives as they moved out in humble, faithful service for Him. With the Lord helping them, they reached their goals. As a senior adult Christians, you and I can trust God for something more than a get-me-by kind of Christianity.

Always remember, *the extremity of your ability is just the beginning of God's opportunity to do something extraordinary* in and through your life. *Don't doubt in the dark what God has told you in the light.* Caleb had some dark days between the promise and the reality, but he never doubted God's Word, and he never lost his passion to serve God faithfully! He ended up standing on the mountain that faith in God and faithfulness to God had provided.

SERVE APPLICATION

What likely caused the disciples not to wash each others' feet before Jesus came to the Upper Room and took on the task Himself?

_____

The disciples called Jesus teacher and Lord. When Jesus repeated those terms, how did He alter the order of those words?

_____

_____

_____

Can we always know in this lifetime whether our service for God is effective or not?

_____Yes

_____No

Who is most important in the Kingdom of God, the person who gives a lot of money to the building program or the one who has little money to give but offers his time to help paint the building to save money for the Church?

_____ The one who gives the most money.

_____ The one who helps paint the church to save money.

_____ The one doing what he/she can with what he/she has.

Approximately how old was Caleb when he took the mountain in the Promised Land that had been promised to him when he was about forty-five years of age?

_____

What three things are needed for us to serve God faithfully?

We need to _____ with God

We need a _____ about God

We need a _____ to God

Caleb left a legacy of God's faithfulness to him and his faithfulness to God by taking the hill country God promised to him and by passing it on to his family. Think of some ways you can leave legacy of service to God for your family and friends and write them below.

_____

_____

_____

Who is the one person in the Bible who left the greatest example of service to the Father?

_____

LEARN

We never reach the point in our Christian lives that we know it all. To be wise in the Lord, is to grow wiser in our knowledge of Him, and His Word, even as we grow older in years. Too many of us automatically equate increased years of living with increased wisdom. Increased years don't necessarily increase good judgment.

A lady named Judy had been at a job for nine years. When a position opened in the company that would mean a promotion and more pay, Judy applied for it. When a younger woman who had only been at the company for two years got the promotion, Judy was furious. She went to her boss and expressed her frustration. "I've been here a long time. I have nine years of experience, and it is not right to give the promotion to someone with only two years of experience," Judy complained.

The boss said, "Judy, you have never grown in your work. Actually, you have one year of experience nine times, but the other lady has grown quickly and has four years of experience in just two years."

Learning means making progress. As Christians, we can repeat the same mistakes for fifty years, or we can learn how to follow God and alter our lives to His will in just a few years. It is not the accumulation of years but the accumulation of wisdom that matters most.

As Christians, we learn a lot of things through experience and/or through the testimony of others; however, we cannot learn to be wise in the Lord without listening to Him and applying His Word, the Bible, to our lives. When we allow Him to speak to us through His Word, He guides us into a closer walk with Him and teaches us how to avoid the traps that Satan places along our paths. We can also learn how to obey God through prayer. When we combine listening to His Word, listening to Him through our experiences, listening to Him through the testimony of others, and listening to Him in faithful prayer, we can learn new things throughout all the years of our lives.

A cursory look at how some older people made progress in the secular world will help us see how open we must be to advancement in our Christian lives as we age. Consider the following:

> Almost all of us have heard of Albert Schweitzer, but few people know that he was still running his hospital in French Equatorial Africa at age eighty-nine.

The great author Leo Tolstoy learned to ride a bicycle at age sixty-seven.

The beautiful Water Lily series of paintings was begun by Claude Monet at age seventy-six.

Elizabeth Arden continued to manage her cosmetics company till she was eighty-six years of age.

Amazingly, Grandma Moses was still painting when she was one hundred years old!

There are many other examples we could consider, but suffice it to say that age does not need to limit our opportunities. There is much we can do if we will simply reject the idea that age determines what we are capable of becoming and doing.

Anna Mary Robertson Moses, known as Grandma Moses, did not begin painting till she was in her seventies. Even when she became famous, she said that she was most proud of her canned preserves and even prouder of her children and grandchildren. Amazingly, when her paintings were opened to the public, she broke attendance records at art museums! A few years ago, long after her death, one of her paintings sold for over one million dollars. I don't think any of her preserves were ever sold at all. And I don't recall ever reading a report about the lives of her children or grandchildren. The point is that we must keep doing our best throughout life. And don't try to judge if your life's work is all that meaningful. We must do what we can, with what we have, where we are, at any age. Only

God can measure the worth of our actions. But we must never think of ourselves as being too old to learn or too old to improve, especially in our walk with God and our service for Him!

In secular education, they have something called lifelong learning. It means to keep improving your knowledge throughout your entire life. Many people retire from their work or vocations and then go back to a community college or university to study something new or advance their knowledge in some field. In the Christian life, we must commit to eternal lifelong learning! By that I mean we have eternal life through faith in Christ, so we must move along a path of learning how to honor the Lord throughout our entire lives. When it comes to our walk with God, we must never think we have arrived at the peak of wisdom. Growing old is something we all must do, unless our years are cut short. Someone once said, "Never despise being old. Always remember that there are many people who never got the privilege." It is important, however, to *grow brighter for the Lord and not to merely grow older in the Lord.* There are some things we can do to ensure that we achieve more in our Christian lives than merely adding years to our biographies. God's Word shares important truths about continuing our growth in the Lord throughout our lives.

BE TEACHABLE

There is an old maxim that states "You can't teach an old dog new tricks." It may be true; I don't know much about teaching tricks to dogs, but I do know that humans, especially Christians, can learn throughout their lives. Christian seniors should never stop learning. It is absolutely untrue that being old keeps us from learning new things, unless we have determined that we simply don't want to learn and improve. Whether in secular life or in the Christian life, one can continue to learn new things throughout life when willing to do so. You can be sure that God's plan includes a lifelong progression of discovery.

I used some secular examples to reveal how people can grow and develop across the years of life, but being open to new things is even more imperative in the Christian life. The world does not stay the same, and though the church is not of the world, the church does exist in the world. Someone wisely said that the church is like a boat; a boat must be in the water, but it never works well to have the water in the boat! We do not want the world in our lives, but we do live and serve Christ in the world. Adapting to the changing culture in which we live can help us effectively serve Jesus. As Christians, we must adapt and grow as the years of life pass; otherwise, we become a burden rather than a blessing to God's work. This means that we must continue to learn how to best serve Christ as we age. Just as we see people in the secular world doing some of their greatest work in their latter years, we can do the same in the Kingdom of God!

WHAT DOES THE BIBLE SAY?

Note a very important Bible verse that teaches us as senior Christians how essential it is to be open to ongoing development.

Better a poor and wise youth

Than an old and foolish king who will be admonished no more.

Ecclesiastes 4:13

This passage is thought provoking, and certainly should be to any aging Christian. The text reveals the danger of being full of pride in old age. This is especially true for an older person who has a position of authority in the church. The danger here is one of being so sure of oneself that you cannot be admonished, corrected, or instructed. The passage goes so far as to state that you would be better off poor and young with enough wisdom to see your need for counsel than to be old and authoritative yet unable to accept advice and direction from others.

NEVER TOO OLD FOR ADVICE

It is interesting to watch golfers and observe their use of a coach throughout their careers. Even the very best golfers in the world have a coach, and some of them have more than one. As they grow older, most golfers who have won numerous tournaments continue to retain a coach to help them with their game. You would think that athletes who are among the top hundred in the world in their field would not need any help, but the very best golfers have coaches. Why? They need a coach to keep them at their best. Their bodies change, the equipment changes, and the golf courses often change as well. The coaches can help the players avoid blind spots, take advantage of improvements in the game, and make adjustments as their bodies change through the years. Sadly, many senior adult Christians feel they have the answer to every situation and find it difficult to accept advice. As a result, they become critical to any variation in the life and work of the church. This can also lead to blind spots in their personal lives. Change is more difficult for us as we age, but Christians must always remain open to God's direction. We must never reach the point in our walk with God that we close our hearts and minds to instruction, correction, or guidance. Many problems arise in our churches due to a sense of ownership that some people insist upon maintaining. We can, if not careful, believe that we have all the answers, and that type of attitude leads many senior leaders in churches to be offended when someone else tries to offer suggestions and advice on the way things are to be done.

CHURCH HISTORY REVEALS CULTURAL CHANGES

I began life in the church when it was considered disrespectful for members to even speak once they entered into a worship service on Sunday morning. Many churches had a portion of Habakkuk 2:20 printed at the bottom of the bulletin: "The Lord is in His holy temple; let all the earth keep silence." That verse was on the bulletin to remind everyone to be quite and respectful once they entered the sanctuary or worship center. As the years passed, changes occurred. Talking, shaking hands, backslapping, and laughter filled the worship center before the actual worship service began. Then a new change was added: everyone was asked by the pastor or worship leader to greet each other in the middle of the service. People walked all over the worship center greeting, hugging, and talking. Finally, another change took place—applause! After a rousing choir anthem or a wonderfully delivered solo, the people in the congregation would applaud. Even in the middle of a sermon, a salient point delivered adroitly by the preacher might illicit a spontaneous applause from the congregation. Many senior Christians were appalled by these changes. Some felt the Lord was being dishonored. Changes such as these caused some senior members to threaten revolt. I remember preachers telling me that some of their members were outraged by these changes in behavior. I must admit that it was difficult being a pastor during those transitional years. Young people were coming to Christ in great numbers, and they had new ideas about how Christ is honored and worshipped. But the older Christians had built the churches with their service and financial gifts, and they felt that they deserved respect and appreciation. Somehow, the senior adult members felt that the changes were not only showing a lack of reverence toward the Lord, but the changes were also evidence of a lack of respect for them and the sacrifices they had made through preceding years. Keeping the two groups in harmony and balance was like juggling watermelons while standing on a tightrope!

Why do we feel so strongly about things that are basically traditional and are not based on specific scriptures or well-defined church doctrine? Frankly, most of us just don't like change, especially if it breaks with what we have found comfortable to us for many years. Certainly tradition has its place, but it can cause us to be unteachable and unwilling to accept change. When the first video screens were placed in a church I pastored, it caused quite a stir. Some thought the devil had put those screens on the walls of the worship center, and all those who thought that were senior adults. As time passed, they came to accept the change as a positive addition to worship.

A willingness to accept change in God's work comes from a heart that is teachable. It is important to guard the sacred Scripture and to adhere to its teachings, but other matters must be open to modification. Reaching people with the Gospel and growing His church is more important than our personal penchant or fondness for a local tradition.

Just think about some of the changes that have occurred in our churches through the years and how easily we accept them today. Our churches used to have hitching posts out front so that people could tie up their horses and buggies when they came to church. Then parking lots were graveled so that automobiles could park without bogging down in the grass or mud. Then paved and lined parking lots were added as more and more people had cars and drove them to church each Sunday. Now there are churches that have parking lots so large that trams or vans are required to pick up the people attending the service because the people attending are parked so far from the entrances that the walk might negatively impact attendance. Churches that had two or more floors for rooms had stairways for attendees to get to the various classrooms. Now there are churches that have escalators and/or elevators. Years ago churches did not have microphones and speakers. Today many churches have massive sound systems, professional video equipment, elaborate lighting systems, coffee shops, bookstores, orchestras, bands, wireless microphones, and every modern convenience available. Many churches now accept credit card and online payment of tithes and offerings!

It is interesting that church members complain about some changes that occur in their churches but rejoice at others. I remember preaching in some churches in the 1960s that did not have air-conditioning. Those summer worship services were brutal! Handheld funeral fans waved in the faces of the members just so they could endure the agonizing heat. From childhood, I remember a few churches that had outhouses for restrooms. When modern air-conditioning and indoor restrooms were added to the buildings, no one complained!

Times have changed, and we have changed with them. There was a time when a man would not think of entering a church without wearing a coat and tie, and a woman would never consider entering the church without wearing a hat and gloves. Now some attendees come to church in khakis and even Bermuda shorts. I must admit that some people, especially young ladies, dress in ways that are not becoming in any public situation, much less in a church; however, the changes in music, clothes, worship styles, and other issues related to worship and church attendance are simply time related. They will change again as time passes. The question is whether we, as senior adult Christians, can be teachable and open to learn new ways to serve God. We must ask ourselves if worship is meant to make us comfortable or if it is an exercise in exalting the Lord and reaching those who need Christ! Sometimes it can be both, but we must always choose that which will win the lost, help the saved to grow in grace, and exalt the Lord.

We must view change in the right light. Often, change provides open doors to reach people that we could not reach before the change occurred. Changes in clothing and music have brought many people into our churches that would not be there otherwise. Always keep in mind that our goal is to live for Christ and to bring people to Him through our witness and testimony. This applies inside and outside the church walls.

WE MUST TAKE ADVANTAGE OF CHANGING TIMES

When my daughter and son were very young, I took them on one of our annual vacations to the mountains of North Carolina. We arrived at the motel, and they immediately began to dress for the swimming pool. I joined them, and we started our short walk to the pool. I noticed that a man had just sat down under one of the umbrellas by the pool and had opened a cooler to take out a beer. I was not happy about my daughter being out there in her swimsuit with some man drinking beer from what appeared to be a full cooler. I mentioned it to my daughter, and she whined, "Oh, Daddy, please, I want to swim!" Just as she said that, God clearly spoke to my heart. The Lord opened my eyes to see that He had placed that man by the pool because He wanted me to talk to him. I was a bit embarrassed by the upbraiding of the Spirit of God, but I accepted it and promptly walked over and asked the man if I could sit down beside him. Interestingly, he asked me if I wanted a beer. It struck me immediately that this gentleman was more willing to offer me what he had than I had been to offer him what I had. I admitted to the man that I didn't drink alcohol, but I would take a soft drink if he had one. He fished around among the beers in his cooler and pulled out a cola for me to drink. I then asked if he knew why I didn't want a beer. He admitted that he was wondering about that. I told him I was a Baptist preacher and didn't drink alcohol due to my commitment to the Lord. I then asked him if he was a Christian. Tears appeared in his eyes as he paused and then said, "No, sir, but my mother was a Christian. She prayed for me a lot. She wanted me to know the Lord and do the right thing." I sat there and shared the plan of salvation with that man by the motel pool. The very thing I was trying to run from, God had placed in front of me as an opportunity for His glory.

As changes occur in our churches and in our world, we can see it as a barrier to our service, or we can view it as an opportunity to find new and better ways to serve Him. God does not live in a box, not even the ones we sometimes create for Him. He is God! He can use us where we are if we are willing to obey Him, serve Him, and honor Him in new ways.

All change is not good, and occasionally we need to speak up, but we must be careful in the process of doing so. It is necessary to consider whether the issue that troubles us is one that really matters when considered in the full scope of God's work. We need to contemplate issues and determine if we are troubled because times are changing, and those changes cause us to feel awkward, or whether a doctrine or scriptural mandate is being abandoned or transgressed. When changes occur that seem to void the validity of God's Word, the saving grace of God's Son, the nature of God, or other doctrinal issues, we must speak up. But when cultural changes occur, we must be willing to accept them and use the opportunities we are given in order to bring people to Christ.

BE EXPANDABLE

Believers should be splendidly growing better and not simply growing older! It is important to acknowledge and recognize that we can follow more closely in the footsteps of Jesus, and that we can allow God to expand us beyond our comfort zones. Being better is not just about avoiding the things we should not do, but it is enlarging and doing better the things that we should do.

QUIT QUITTING

There is a story about a revival that took place many years ago. It was called a quitting meeting. The evangelist shared messages about the social sins of the day and asked people to quit doing the things that offended the Lord. Those attending were asked to make a public commitment of their willingness to recommit their lives by laying aside the sins that so easily beset them. On the final day of the meeting, each person was asked to come forward and lay down those sinful ways. One man came and said, "I have been drinking, and I hereby resign that way of life. I will quit drinking henceforth and not allow liquor to cross the lips with which I praise God." The people shouted, "Amen!" Then a woman came forward and said, "I have been dipping snuff, and I will throw it out when I get home and will not allow that nasty stuff to be placed in my mouth again as long as I live." Great shouts of praise went up from the congregation. Others made similar commitments. One lady who was known to be pious and a bit self-righteous got so caught up in the rededications that she jumped up and said, "I ain't been doing nothing, and I pledge to quit quitting right here and now!"

Many of us need to quit quitting; that is, we need to start doing the things we are supposed to do. We must allow God to expand our horizons and be willing for Him to test us in greater and larger ways.

PRESS ON

There is no doubt that most of us can be better and do better in our lives for Christ! Many people think that the Christian life is mostly concerned with the things we are not to do. Certainly, there is some truth to that; however, it is just as important that we know what we are to be doing and get on with doing it. Christian living is not just a life of not doing bad things; the Christian life is about doing the right things. In Matthew 25, when our Lord condemned some to eternal separation from God, He said it was because they "*did it not.*" It was not what they had done wrong that He judged, but chiefly it was what they *had not done that condemned them*! The judgment that Jesus pronounced was due to the things left undone. We often look at sin as being the bad or evil things that people do. Jesus pointed out in Matthew 25 that it is a terrible sin to leave undone those things that God tells us to do! Things we do that are in violation of God's prohibitions are called *sins of commission*, but the things we fail to do are known as *sins of omission*. Our Lord pointed out that an eternal danger lies in the sins of omission—the things left undone!

Listen to the attitude of Paul on the matter of making progress in serving God:

> Yet indeed I also count all things loss for the excellence of the knowledge of Christ Jesus my Lord, for whom I have suffered the loss of all things, and count them as rubbish, that I may gain Christ and be found in Him, not having my own righteousness, which *is* from the law, but that which *is* through faith in Christ, the righteousness which is from God by faith; that I may know Him and the power of His resurrection, and the fellowship of His sufferings, being conformed to His death, if, by any means, I may attain to the resurrection from the dead. Not that I have already attained, or am already perfected; but I press on, that I may lay hold of that for which Christ Jesus has also laid hold of me. Brethren, I do not count myself to have apprehended; but one thing *I do,* forgetting those things which are behind and reaching forward to those things which are ahead, I press toward the goal for the prize of the upward call of God in Christ Jesus. Therefore let us, as many as are mature,

have this mind; and if in anything you think otherwise, God will reveal even this to you. Nevertheless, to *the degree* that we have already attained, let us walk by the same rule, let us be of the same mind.

Philippians 3:8–16

Note that Paul's desire was to press on in his quest to attain a greater knowledge of Christ and to reach the goal that God had for him in his life. In other words, no matter what Paul had accomplished, he counted it as nothing compared to his desire to be better, to know Christ better, and to serve Him better. He even went so far as to say that he in no way considered himself to have attained the spiritual level that God had for him. Paul was not talking about being saved; he was speaking of being his best for Jesus! It was this attitude that helped propel Paul forward, even into his later years, with an enthusiasm and animation that shook the world for Christ. Paul wanted to expand his service and devotion to the Lord. He was not satisfied with the status quo in his service for Jesus.

For many of us, the fire and desire for expanding our service to Christ is missing, especially as we get older. We settle down and begin to think that we have done our work, and it is time for someone else to do it now. Certainly, we need to allow others to have places of service for the Lord through the years, but we must never think we have arrived when it comes to serving Christ. There is much for us to learn and much for us to do. We can be better. Don't you agree?

GET OUT OF THE RUT

To be expandable means to get out of the rut and find new ways of serving the Lord. It is not just doing better what we already do, but asking God if there are new ways He wishes to use us in His service. The group that Jesus had the most trouble with when He was on earth was the Pharisees and those like them who thought they had everything figured out. They were not able to expand their horizons and missed their chance to serve the Messiah. We must not let that happen to us. Ask God if there are new places and ways of service that you need to discover. It may surprise you to find a greater joy in your senior years of service to God than you had in your younger days.

BE FLEXIBLE

I became pastor of the First Baptist Church, Lilburn, Georgia, in 1990. The church had been through some tough times, had gone through a split of its membership, and had declined in Sunday school to the point that attendance had dipped into the four hundreds. The church was in debt, the buildings were in disarray, and grass was growing up through the broken pavement in the parking lot. Needless to say, I didn't want to become pastor there at that time. But the Lord pressed me in my heart and soul that it was His will for me to accept the call of the church to be their pastor. Once I was pastor of the church, I found a congregation of wonderful people with a deep love for Jesus. In fact, I noted immediately that they were some of the finest Christian people I had ever known. I prayed fervently for God's direction in those first four to six weeks concerning the vision God had for us. After only three months as their pastor, I asked the church to gather for a State of the Church Address. I was prepared to tell them what God had placed on my heart for us as a church. I wasn't excited about it because I knew what I had to say could spell my doom; I feared my wife would have to repack our belongings and that we would have to find a new place to go following that meeting. But I did what I knew God wanted and addressed a packed church that Sunday evening. After listing some basic things, I came to the part that I knew would be tough for the church to accept. I told them I believed the Lord wanted us to build a new building and update our grounds and surroundings in order to reach new people. Remember, the church was in debt, had little money, and I was the only full-time ministerial staff member. It was a bold thing I placed before them that night. An older retired preacher we lovingly called Preacher James was a member of the church, and he stood and asked, "Preacher, may I address the congregation?" My heart fluttered. If that distinguished and respected man said that my vision was flawed, the entire dream would explode before it even began. I told him that he most certainly could address the church. Preacher James slowly walked to the podium. With a voice that sounded like he just stepped out of the presence of the Almighty, he said, "Brothers and sisters, in all my years of ministry, I have never heard a word more clearly sent from the throne of God than we have just heard from our pastor. We should rise and follow our pastor as one!" The congregation stood in a resounding applause.

We were on our way! The building was erected in a matter of eighteen months and was entirely paid for in seven years. New staff members were added. Computers, equipment, and other needed items were purchased. New signs and updated landscaping graced the property. People began joining immediately. In a short period, we were averaging nine hundred in Sunday school and over 1,100 in worship each week. This would not have happened had it not been for that retired senior adult pastor who stood with me that night in 1990 and those bold church members who were not afraid of pressing on to a greater and brighter future.

I have thought about that night many times in the intervening years. Surely it took courage and faith for that man to stand with me as his new pastor. After all, he hardly knew me. I had only been his pastor for three months, and I had only spoken with him a few times. But he stood up that night and gave his assent to a vision that could have made us both look foolish had it failed. But he was flexible and willing to accept change. He was willing to trust God, and he did not concern himself with the impediments that stood before us as a congregation. Often, as senior adult Christians, we depend too much on what we think we know and not enough on who God is and what God can do. I know we need to use common sense in our decisions, but we must keep our focus on the greatness of God and remain flexible in the light of His will.

LIKE A TREE IN THE WIND

It is possible for God to bend and shape us through faith. A tree can only last in the wind if it is flexible. I am sure you have seen trees bending wildly in a storm that is accompanied by strong winds. When that happens, we often wonder how the trees can withstand such tremendous gusts of wind. Trees that are flexible stand a much better chance of survival and success than those that are rigid and stiff. Likewise, the Christian that is flexible can stand stronger and longer in the winds of change that come in life than those that are too rigid. Being flexible does not mean compromising our beliefs; it means committing ourselves to the God of heaven who is able to work in new ways to bring about His will.

Note what Paul said about being flexible:

> For though I am free from all men, I have made myself a servant to all, that I might win the more; and to the Jews I became as a Jew, that I might win Jews; to those who are under the law, as under the law, that I might win those who are under the law; to those who are without law, as without law (not being without law toward God, but under law toward Christ), that I might win those who are without law; to the weak I became as weak, that I might win the weak. I have become all things to all men, that I might by all means save some.

> 1 Corinthians 9:19–22

Paul did not say that he forfeited his standards in order to conform to the world or the ideas of man;

what Paul stated was a willingness to forgo his personal preferences in order that he might see people come to know Christ as Lord and Savior. Paul was well aware that he could not win all the people to Christ nor could he win most people to Christ, but by being flexible in his attitudes and actions, he could win some people to Christ. Paul was willing to adapt his way of life to fit a plan that would bring people into fellowship with Jesus. Paul's willingness to be flexible made him one of the greatest Christian servants in history.

IT IS NOT ABOUT ME!

In order to serve the Lord faithfully and win people to faith in Jesus, we must be willing to lay aside some of our personal proclivities and inclinations. Churches have been divided and practically ruined by members who argued vehemently over things as trivial as the kind of light fixture to be used in a renovation project, or the color of new carpet for some portion of the buildings. As senior adult Christians, we must show an example of flexibility in all matters that do not relate to salvation or compulsory doctrine.

This same attitude applies to areas outside the church. In our home and among friends, we need to have a sweet spirit and exhibit a loving attitude. We will never agree with everyone on everything, but we can show a tenderness of heart that reveals the Spirit of God within us. Our witness is affected by the attitude we share in daily life. In fact, how we act at the grocery store or toward a waitperson in a restaurant can reflect positively or negatively on our witness for Christ. How we treat our family members in our homes can make a difference throughout the generations that follow us in the service of Christ. Determine that you will be flexible and willing to accept change so that you can be useable in God's service.

LEARN APPLICATION (ANSWERS)
The best knowledge in life for a Christian comes from two things. What are they?

_____

_____

If we do not adapt to changes that occur during our lifetime, we become a _____ rather than a _____ to God's Work.

As change occurs, we want to be sure that we do two things effectively. What are they?

_____

_____

Christians can always become more _____ as they grow older.

The Christian life is not just about not doing things that are wrong. It is also about _____.

Paul was a great Christian servant, but he wrote that it was his desire to _____on in his quest to_____all that God meant for Him to be and do.

In 1 Corinthians 9:23, Paul stated that he was never willing to accept changes to his personal preferences in order to win people to Christ.

_____ True

_____ False

A tree that survives a storm of mighty winds is one that has one characteristic. What is it?

_____

REST

A small newspaper was having problems with subscriptions. In order to boost sales, the editor decided to begin a contest. A search began for the laziest man in the newspaper readership area. A prize of $5,000 would be given to the man chosen. The idea worked. Subscriptions rose rapidly as people followed the ongoing search for the laziest man around. Finally, the week came for the announcement of the winner. The editor and a photographer went out in the country to award the prize and get a photograph of the winner. They arrived at a rundown cabin in the woods and were greeted by a disheveled woman standing on a porch that was clearly leaning to one side. They asked how they might find the man in question, and she told them that he was her husband and that he was down at the creek. After getting directions, they struck out through the woods to find him. They came upon the man down by the creek lying flat on his back with a straw hat over his eyes. A fishing pole was stuck in the ground beside him with a line running out into the creek. The fishing line was floating on top of the water. It was apparent that the fishing line had no weight or hook on it. Clearly the lazy man did not wish to be bothered by some busy fish grabbing the line. The editor asked, "Sir, are you Bill Beakins?" The old man answered, "Yep." Of course, Lazy Bill did not even attempt to remove the hat that covered his eyes. The editor told Bill that he was the laziest-man-contest winner, and they had a check for him made out for $5,000. Bill never moved; he simply said in a slow drawl, "Roll me over, boys, and put the check in my back pocket!"

When we consider the subject of rest, we are not thinking of Bill Beakins! Neither is the rest I want you to consider the causal afternoon nap we sometimes need and enjoy as senior adults; rather, the rest we will examine in this chapter is the biblical concept of being content—at peace or rest in the Lord.

Life is filled with responsibilities and duties. Frustrations arise constantly. If we do not know or follow God's guidelines for contentment, we can become utterly exasperated with life. The incidence of prescription drug abuse in the United States is at a dangerous level. People do need medications at times in order to cope with overwhelming situations, but the use of drugs for mood alteration is accelerating. Christians need to know God's prescription for overcoming anxiety, worry, and depression.

In Philippians 4, Paul addresses this issue in a personal way and calls upon all of us to discover the path to experiencing rest in the Lord. By resting, Paul is not talking about the absence of activity. He is speaking about rest from worry and anxiety in the midst of life's difficulties. Many senior adults discover that age brings with it a struggle to avoid being overly worried about things that are basically unimportant or unchangeable. Looking at God's Word and applying the principles found there can help us obtain victory over anxiety, and in turn, that will produce a more effective and enjoyable life for us and those around us.

To be sure, a normal amount of apprehension about the issues of life is necessary. Increased emotional concern can help us avoid dangerous situations, guard against unscrupulous people, and keep us on our toes; however, unnecessary intensification of our nervous system can harm us in many ways. If we become too content, we simply become lazy and indifference. If we become overanxious, we become weak and ineffective in every area of our lives.

We are concerned at this point in our study with finding God's rest and peace in the midst of life's experiences, especially those related to aging. Jesus said to His disciples,

> Peace I leave with you, My peace I give to you; not as the world gives do I give to you. Let not your heart be troubled, neither let it be afraid.
>
> John 14:27

Jesus does not offer the kind of peace the world suggests—a false peace based on earthly possessions, health, friends, money, etc. God's peace is based on something entirely different. In fact, God's peace is so sure and authentic that once you discover how to apply it to your life, nothing can take it from you. Paul wrote:

> Not that I speak in regard to need, for I have learned in whatever state I am, to be content: I know how to be abased, and I know how to abound. Everywhere and in all things I have learned both to be full and to be hungry, both to abound and to suffer need.
>
> Philippians 4:11–12

Paul had learned to rest in the Lord. It did not matter whether he had more than he needed or less than he needed; he was content in either situation. When he experienced comfortable surroundings, he did not trust the things he had. He knew how easy it would be for him to lose those things. When he had very little, he did not worry that he might starve or die because he knew that God owned everything and his needs would be met. Paul did not know God's rest and peace as a theory; he knew it from experience.

We need to take a moment to consider some reasons that worry is not good for us; in fact, an overabundance of worry can be classified as a sin. Jesus spoke clearly about this:

> Therefore I say to you, do not worry about your life, what you will eat or what you will drink; nor about your body, what you will put on. Is not life more than food and the body more than clothing? Look at the birds of the air, for they neither sow nor reap nor gather into barns;

yet your heavenly Father feeds them. Are you not of more value than they? Which of you by worrying can add one cubit to his stature?

So why do you worry about clothing? Consider the lilies of the field, how they grow: they neither toil nor spin; and yet I say to you that even Solomon in all his glory was not arrayed like one of these. Now if God so clothes the grass of the field, which today is, and tomorrow is thrown into the oven, will He not much more clothe you, O you of little faith?

Therefore do not worry, saying, "What shall we eat?" or "What shall we drink?" or "What shall we wear?" For after all these things the Gentiles seek. For your heavenly Father knows that you need all these things. But seek first the kingdom of God and His righteousness, and all these things shall be added to you. Therefore do not worry about tomorrow, for tomorrow will worry about its own things. Sufficient for the day is its own trouble.

Matthew 6:25–34

These words from Jesus don't need a lot of commentary. Jesus knew that a certain measure of concern was necessary in the process of living through any given day on this earth. He told us that each day will have its *own trouble*. But He clearly told us not to *worry*. Why was Jesus concerned about His followers worrying?

Worry Harms Our Bodies

We know today that worry increases the likelihood of illness and increases the damage of illnesses we are already experiencing. Somewhere I read a story a few years ago about a woman who was prone to worry too much about every minor physical problem that arose. Her children called her a hypochondriac. One day she was knitting, and one of her fingers became stiff and painful. She opened her medical dictionary and found the section on arthritis. She continued to read for some time and came across information about the worst kinds of joint disease. As she read, she became convinced that she was in the deep stages of rheumatoid arthritis. In fact, by the time she finished reading, both of her hands were in pain and curved into claws. The lady rushed to the doctor's office, claimed an emergency, and got in to see her family physician. She explained what had happened to her. The doctor asked, "Just how did you come to think that you have advanced arthritis?" She replied, "I read it in my medical dictionary!" The doctor nodded and proceeded to write out a prescription. He folded it, handed it to her, and said, "This should take care of your problem."

The lady rushed as quickly as she could to the pharmacy and handed the attendant the prescription. In a few moments, the pharmacist came to the counter and said, "Ma'am, I can't help you with this. Just read it yourself."

The lady opened the prescription, and this is what her doctor had written: "You don't have a serious problem—just stop reading medical dictionaries, and you will be fine!"

Psychosomatic disease is a problem, and we know more about that today than ever in history. The mind plays tricks on our bodies. If we do not think as we should, we can make small issues much bigger than they really are. In short, worry is not good for your health.

I preached a revival at the First Baptist Church in Welcome, North Carolina, a number of years ago. One night I spoke on the subject of worry. During the invitation, an elderly lady came forward. I noticed that the pastor spent a great deal of time with her. When the invitation ended, the pastor presented the lady to the church as a new believer. He explained that she had been a member of the church for decades but that she realized during the worship service that she had never really trusted Christ as her Savior. The church rejoiced over her decision to trust Jesus, and the service ended. Immediately, her husband came to me and said something like this: "Preacher, I have known for years that my wife couldn't really be a Christian. She worried too much to be saved. She worried about everything and did it all the time."

After the revival, I returned to my own church to continue my ministry. One day my phone rang, and the daughter of the elderly lady who had made the decision for Christ was on the other end of the line. She told me what happened after that worship service. She said, "My mother thought she had some disease that was going to kill her every day for the last forty years. Well, a few weeks after the revival, she had a stroke and was taken to the hospital. This time she was really sick. The doctors were not even sure if she was going to make it. Yet every time the doctor came to see her, she begged him to go home. She would say, 'I'm all right. I'm not that sick. God will take care of me. Let me go home.'"

What had changed in the life that of eighty-plus-year-old woman? She had found peace in Christ. She was at *rest*. She was no longer worried about her health. Prior to committing her life fully to Christ, she worried about things that didn't even exist. After receiving Jesus into her life, she was convinced that no matter what happened, she was going to be okay.

No one has a right to be sicker than he or she ought to be! Yes, sometimes we are really sick, and we need medical attention and special care. And yes, it is okay to have a normal amount of concern about the treatment of our bodies. But it is inappropriate to worry to the point of obsession about our health. Jesus told us not to do that. It is a sin for us to do so! And it is counterproductive to the healing process for whatever is going on in our bodies.

WORRY HINDERS OUR WITNESS

It is impossible to be incessantly worried and be a proper witness for Christ at the same time. Every Christian has the privilege and duty of sharing his or her faith with others, but who would be interested in joining you in trusting Jesus if you are constantly complaining about your worries and anxieties? When we cannot rest in Christ, we present a poor witness concerning the peace that Jesus gives those who trust in Him.

Imagine for a moment that you are talking to a neighbor who needs to know Jesus, or to someone who is simply not participating in the worship and service of a local church. As you speak to your neighbor, you say, "I'm so worried. I'm just a nervous wreck thinking that I might be laid off from my job. I don't know what I would do. And by the way, I'm troubled to death about my sister's health. She is not doing well, and I can't stop thinking the worst. And while I'm at it, let me tell you that I'm in a dither about my son's marriage. It is keeping me up at night worrying about what is going to happen to my family." Then just as you complete those sentences, you remember that you have been looking for an opportunity to invite this neighbor to attend your church, so you add, "Oh, by the way, would you like to come to church with me on Sunday?"

I can assure you that your neighbor does not wish to go to your church. After all, if your Lord, your worship, and your church leave you so worried and anxious that you can't sleep at night, why would your neighbor wish to be involved? Most people have enough troubles of their own without going to a church where the members are worried to death about the issues of life.

Worry and anxiety damage your witness. It causes people to doubt that Jesus makes any difference in your life or can make any difference in their lives. When we display a sense of divine peace in the midst of life's storms, it causes people to wonder just how we can remain so calm and at rest. In fact, there are times when people will ask, "How can you be so calm when you are dealing with some many problems?" A question like that presents a marvelous opportunity for us to tell people that our peace and rest come from the Lord Jesus Christ!

WORRY HALTS OUR FAITH

It is impossible to have faith and be filled with worry at the same time. We dealt somewhat with faith in a previous chapter, but at this point, we need to consider how faith relates to relieving anxiety.

In Hebrews 11:6, we read, "But without faith it is impossible to please Him, for he who comes to God must believe that He is, and that He is a rewarder of those who diligently seek Him." Wow! Did you read closely what that verse clearly states? Without faith, one *cannot please God*. Every believer has a desire to please God, but when we worry due to a lack of faith, it is impossible to please Him. Worry and faith are contradictory moods or attitudes. It is difficult to justify the following statement: "I trust God completely, but I am worried to death."

God means for you to place your faith in Him and to trust Him fully. That is why Jesus told us that we are to *seek first the kingdom of God* and place the other issues in God's hands. Instead of worrying over a dozen issues, we can look to Him and make that our only concern.

I know you have heard of a consolidated loan, which is used in order to take several debts and combine them into one single debt. When someone does this, it is often to lessen the amount they pay every month and to reduce the number of checks they have to write each month. In a way, God is asking His children to consolidate their worries. Take all your issues and give them to Him and then just concentrate on pleasing God each day. If you will trust Him, He promises to make sure the other issues are worked out satisfactorily. This takes faith, but when it is practiced, it reduces your stress and increases your peace.

Pointing out how wrong it is to worry is easy to do, but discovering how we can overcome anxiety is the real problem. To discover the requirements for overcoming worry and anxiety, let's turn back to Paul and the principles he gave us in his letter to the Philippians. Paul revealed three stages in overcoming anxiety. If we will learn them and practice them, we can find the peace and contentment that God means for us to enjoy. Let's look at these three stages and consider how we can use them to help us be *senior Christians living super lives* for our Lord.

PRAY CORRECTLY

We now consider how to find peace with God, His wonderful, divine rest, through praying correctly. Yes, you can pray incorrectly and ineffectively. That may seem strange to you, but it is a fact. The disciples knew that this was true. Once they came to Jesus and asked Him to teach them to pray. Why would they need to be taught to pray unless there was a right way and wrong way to do so? Also, when they asked Jesus how to pray, He did not tell them that instruction in this practice was unnecessary. In fact, he proceeded to help them with the issue of praying correctly. When it comes to anxiety, Paul gave some clear instructions on how to pray properly in order to obtain peace.

> Be anxious for nothing, but in everything by prayer and supplication, with thanksgiving, let your requests be made known to God; and the peace of God, which surpasses all understanding, will guard your hearts and minds through Christ Jesus.
>
> Philippians 4:6–7

Clearly we are told in Philippians 4:6 that we are to be *anxious for nothing*, which means *not to be anxious about anything*. This is an imperative statement, meaning that it is a command. It is easy to command something, but that does not mean it is necessarily easy for people to obey; however, Paul goes on to tell us how to comply with this command. Knowing how to avoid anxiety may be one of the best-kept secrets in the Bible. It is plainly written by Paul, and it is implied in numerous other verses in the Bible, yet many Christians never discover it.

Archbishop Trench was a New Testament scholar. He wrote *Synonyms of the New Testament*, which was—and still is—very popular among Christian theologians and Christians in general. A story has circulated for years about the bishop, and it is worth recalling.

Even though Trench was a dedicated saint and a great scholar, he became worried and persuaded that he was losing the use of his limbs and the feeling in his legs. One evening he was at a very posh state dinner seated with distinguished guests. In the middle of the dinner, he cried out, "Oh, it finally happened. It's finally happened. I haven't got a bit of feeling in my right leg." The lady sitting next to him said, "Your grace, if it will be any comfort to you, it's my leg you're pinching!" Needless to say, it was a most embarrassing moment brought on by the archbishop's overabundant worry and anxiety. From this incident, we can see that even the best and brightest Christians find it difficult to overcome worry and find true rest in Christ.

In order for us to find the peace Christ intends, we must pray the way Paul described in our text from Philippians.

PRAY WITH THANKSGIVING

Paul declared that we are to take everything to God through prayer, but he added that it must be done with *thanksgiving.* Don't miss this point, or you will never learn the secret to prayer that leads to rest in Christ. You need to be reminded that Paul wrote the passage we are considering from Philippians while he was in a Roman jail. He was not writing from a carpeted pastor's study. He did not pen these words while at the beach on sabbatical. He was in a situation that had no assurance of a positive outcome. He knew that the Romans could put him to death any time they decided to do so. Yet he wrote these encouraging and wonderful instructions regarding the peace of God from a Roman prison. It is easy to be upbeat when everything in life is going your way, but it requires something special to be joyful and at rest when danger is lurking around every corner of your life. Paul had the peace and rest he needed to overcome his circumstances, and he shares in this text how we can have this peace as well. Paul knew that one of the things necessary to overcome worry and anxiety was *thanksgiving*.

Why is thanksgiving so important in prayer? Thanksgiving is the result of some previous blessing that God has provided in our lives. You give thanks to God because He has done something for you. Thus, Paul is telling us that we must thank God for something He has already done for us before we tell Him what we are dealing with at the moment. By remembering the answers to previous prayers and God's intervention to deliver us from prior circumstances, we are brought to a point of renewed and energized faith. Let me give you an example.

When I was in my early thirties, a doctor examined me and called me in for a meeting. He asked that my wife come with me. We knew that he would not ask both of us to attend this conference in his office unless the issue to be discussed was serious. In the meeting, he informed us that it was extremely likely from the results of his tests that I had an aggressive cancer that could be deadly. He stated that I needed surgery immediately. The surgery was planned to take place as soon as it was possible. Needless to say, we were in a state of shock. We had two young children and were looking forward to a full life together. We prayed about this and asked others to pray with us.

The surgery took place, and my wife and others waited in the hospital visitor's area for the results. The doctor came out and told my wife that he was totally surprised to find that the suspicious mass was nothing but tissue. There was either no cancer present in my body, or God had healed me. Either way, joy filled us all as we got the news!

That was almost forty years ago, but it is still fresh in my mind. When I pray about something troubling me deeply today, I always go back to that incident, and I thank God again and again for sparing my life. Sure, the news could have been different, and one day it likely will be different for me. Certainly for everyone who goes through tests and surgery, the news is not always positive. But on that one occasion, it was good news for me and for my family. So when I pray about something serious, I go back in my mind and thank God over and over again for delivering me through that experience. To this day, it often brings me to tears as I thank the Lord for His blessings in that situation. I praise Him that I have seen my children grow into adults. I thank Him that I now have four grandchildren and two great-grandchildren. I exalt Him for all the years of ministry He has allowed me to enjoy since that surgery. Only then do I make my request regarding any present-day difficulty I am facing. In fact, once I begin to thank God for the good news He gave us following that biopsy, I begin to think of all the other wonderful things God has done for me. I praise Him for bringing me through accidents, a tour of duty in Vietnam in the 1960s, and many other perils that He has brought my family through. As I thank Him for previous blessings, my present faith in increased. As I thank Him, my trust in Him is enlarged. My present circumstances don't seem so immense because I am recalling that He is bigger than any problem I have ever had in my life.

Only after I have thanked Him do I present my current request. In fact, after I have thanked the Lord for numerous blessings from the past, I sometimes have to stop a moment to remember what my current problem actually is. You see, when you get into an attitude of gratitude for all that God has done, it overshadows your current problems. No, it doesn't make your present problem disappear, but it does cover it with faith in God. Once you have praised God for countless blessings, you can bring your immediate need to Him with faith that He will not fail you. This step begins the process of lessening the effect of worry and anxiety in the heart of a Christian. When I am reminded of God's blessings and how much He loves me, I know I can trust Him with whatever I am going through at the moment.

When you are facing difficult situations, you will not find *rest* in your spirit if you concentrate on the difficulty to the exclusion of recalling the blessings God has given you in the past. Don't fall on your knees and start complaining about how bad things are in your life without taking time to thank God for delivering you through so many obstacles in the past. Praise Him. Worship Him. Thank Him. This keeps you from turning your prayer time into a *pity party.* So many people pray in such a negative way that the prayer adds to their anxieties. If you bring requests to God in the wrong way, it can actually make you more nervous than you were before you prayed! You see, once you repeat a problem in prayer, it solidifies in your mind just how bad the situation is. Turn that around. Pray with faith. Pray with thanksgiving. Spend more time thanking God than you do telling Him about the problem you have. Yes, He wants you to bring your concerns and troubles to Him, but He is not a human counselor—He is *God!* Do this correctly, and you will feel the weight of your present problem being immediately lifted from your heart, mind, and spirit. Doing this puts you in the right frame of mind, in the arena of faith, and in the place of expectation as you pray.

PRAY WITH REQUESTS

Once you have reminded yourself and God of the answered prayers and blessings from the past, bring your requests to Him. The word *requests* in this text speaks of *specific* rather than *general* supplication. We don't have to tell the Lord every detail of the problem; He already knows what you need before you ask Him (Matthew 6:8), but we must be specific. When you mention your requests, be pointed. Tell the Lord what you need Him to do. When I prayed about the diagnosis of cancer, my prayer was "God, spare me through this so I can raise my family and continue to preach your Word. I want to honor you. If cancer honors you, then I will deal with it, but I ask you to spare me through this so I can carry out my duties to you and to my family." We can't tell God what to do, in spite of what some television preachers say on the subject. I don't have the authority to tell God, "You have to cure me. I am trusting you, and I come in the name of Jesus to tell you to make me well. I am praying in faith and according to your Word, so you have to do it!" That is not biblical. God's will may involve elements that I cannot see. His purpose may be worked out in ways different from my own desires. My prayer is simply to tell God where I am and that I wish to honor Him through it. Praying in this manner places me in the position of peace. I can rest once I have laid it before Him with thanksgiving. He loves me. He will not fail me. Certainly praying in this manner does not mean that everything will turn out the way I want it to, but I know God will do what is best. He loves me. He has blessed me in the past. He has kept me alive all these years for a purpose. I thank Him and then leave it with Him. That is true rest in Christ!

I have prayed for things that turned out differently than I requested. Surely you have done the same. But as we look back, we can see that God was leading us in His path, for His glory, and for our best. In other words, we must never view God as a cosmic Santa Claus. We are not trying to turn God into a heavenly Tooth Fairy. God is not my bellhop. He is God! My concern is to act in faith, to honor Him, and to find the place of peace and rest in my heart and soul. That is what we can have if we pray with thanksgiving while letting our requests rest with God. Peter put it like this: "Casting all your care upon Him, for He cares for you" (1 Peter 5:7).

Paul even tells us the results of this kind of praying. He states clearly that the *peace of God* will be with us. Isn't that what we want after all? Paul had been through experiences that were far beyond anything the average Christian will ever face in life. He had learned how to pray in order to have the *peace of God* in all circumstances. In the following passage, we read some of the things Paul faced in his service for God:

> Are they Hebrews? So am I. Are they Israelites? So am I. Are they the seed of Abraham? So am I. Are they ministers of Christ? I speak as a fool—I am more: in labors more abundant, in stripes above measure, in prisons more frequently, in deaths often. From the Jews five times I received forty stripes minus one. Three times I was beaten with rods; once I was stoned; three times I was shipwrecked; a night and a day I have been in the deep; in journeys often, in perils of waters, in perils of robbers, in perils of my own countrymen, in perils of the Gentiles, in perils in the city, in perils in the wilderness, in perils in the sea, in perils among false brethren; in weariness and toil, in sleeplessness often, in hunger and thirst, in fastings often, in cold and nakedness—besides the other things, what comes upon me daily: my deep concern for all the churches.
>
> 2 Corinthians 11:22–29

Paul knew hardships, and he had found the way to have rest in the midst of them. He had learned the path to the *peace of God* that was beyond understanding. That, in fact, is exactly what we need—a peace that we cannot understand. We need to find a way for our minds to *rest* even when we are going through troubles of many kinds. Praying the right way leads to that kind of rest and peace.

Paul told us that the peace of God would guard our hearts and minds in Christ Jesus. You don't need a guard on something unless the thing being guarded is valuable. You lock your house when you leave home, and you probably keep it locked when you are at home. You lock your car. Why? You lock things up because they are valuable and you wish to protect them. Our hearts and minds are susceptible to worry, anxiety, and troubled thoughts. These rob us, as we have already seen. When we pray as we should, it brings us into a closer fellowship with our Lord, and this provides a garrison around our hearts and minds so that the evil one cannot plant the seeds of apprehension and agitation inside. Paul had seen the Roman garrisons as they guarded strategic places in the Roman Empire. He knew that an enemy would have to face these fierce Roman soldiers if they desired to get into the heart of a city or compound. Likewise, Paul tells us that God will put a garrison on our hearts and minds if we pray about our problems in the proper manner. God promises us a peace in Jesus so great that Satan and his minions have to face the garrisons of God in order to invade our minds with worry and anxiety, and you can be sure that Christ is greater than all your enemies.

Pray correctly. You will discover a new joy and peace, even in the midst of hardship and trouble. Pray with thanksgiving, and pray with trust! You will find that you worry less, witness better, have more joy, live in peace, and experience increased energy for the things that really matter in life.

THINK RIGHTLY

Praying correctly will not solve the entire problem of worry and anxiety. We can't remain in prayer at every moment of every day. Since this is true, we must deal with the issue of our thinking after we have prayed. In order to find real *rest* in our minds and spirits, we must *think* correctly. We can be guilty of *stinking thinking*, which is nothing more than filling our minds with thoughts that are counterproductive to God's peace. Paul provides us with a list of thoughts that should occupy our minds.

> Finally, brethren, whatever things are true, whatever things are noble, whatever things are just, whatever things are pure, whatever things are lovely, whatever things are of good report, if there is any virtue and if there is anything praiseworthy—meditate on these things.
>
> Philippians 4:8

Note that all of the thoughts Paul mentioned in Philippians 4:8 are positive thoughts. Paul was pointing out that God's people have the presence of the Lord and the promises of the Lord, and therefore, we should keep our minds fixed on good thoughts. Let's take a moment and consider these words from their original meanings.

TRUE

This word speaks of *not concealing*. In fact, the Greek word used by Paul is a negative article fused with the word *conceal*. It means to be open and honest. We are to be above board in our behavior and speech. We are never to pat a person on the back and then roast that person verbally once he or she is out of sight. We must speak the truth in love (Ephesians 4:15) so that we might grow up in the Lord. If you are double-minded, you will never be filled with peace. You cannot act one way and think another and have peace at the same time. What is in your mind will work its way to the surface of your life. Be true to God and to yourself. This creates added peace.

NOBLE

This word means to speak that which is *honorable*. We are to speak words that bring honor to God and to others. When we think and speak things that are base and insulting, we dishonor God and open our hearts and minds to tension and anxiety. Keep your mind above the gutter level of life. Honorable thinking brings rest in one's mind and heart.

JUST

God desires that we think thoughts that are innocent. This means to keep our minds from thinking negative thoughts about God or others. Jesus told us not to judge because we will then be judged by God with the same judgment we use against others. Many times we *judge* the actions or motives of others without all the facts (Matthew 7:1–5). When people judge us in the same manner, we feel harmed because we know things about our actions that others do not know. When we judge people, we open our minds to Satan who is called the *accuser*. In Zechariah 3:1–3, we see Satan accusing Joshua before the angel of the Lord. Satan accused

Job before the Lord as well. We must not enter into a pact with Satan by becoming accusers of people in our minds or with our words. You cannot have peace of mind if you spend your time judging others.

PURE

The word *pure* means to be clean. This is a struggle for every Christian, but it is a struggle we must win. It is important to keep our thoughts chaste and pure. Impure thoughts form pathways into our hearts and minds, and this opens us up to anxiety. Having *rest* in Christ requires maintaining a pure mind. We cannot keep an evil thought from passing through our head, but we can keep it from setting up a home in our mind. If you entertain evil thoughts, you will open up your life to increased anxiety.

LOVELY

This speaks of thinking *friendly* thoughts. The word *lovely* in our text comes from the word *pro* (toward) and the word *friendly*. It means to keep friendly thoughts toward people. It can also mean to maintain *lovely* thoughts about life in general.

A preacher friend of mine had a couple in his church that avoided him from the first day he arrived to lead that church. He and his wife both experienced this behavior from the couple. He knew of no reason for their attitude of rejection. His first thought was to simply avoid them as well, but he knew that kind of thinking would only lead to problems, so he and his wife discussed it and decided on a plan. They made it a goal to personally speak to this couple every time they saw them. Even if the couple turned to go in another direction to avoid them, the preacher and his wife would practically chase them down and make them engage in a conversation. He befriended them every way he could. Within a few months, the couple became friends with the pastor and his wife. When the pastor left the church for another place of service, that couple wept and said, "Never in our lives have we had a preacher and preacher's wife like you. We will never forget you." The pastor and his wife simply thought *lovely* thoughts toward that couple and won their affection. This kept the pastor and his wife from being anxious about this couple, and it kept them from filling their minds with negative thoughts about one of the families in their congregation. Don't allow Satan to plant unfriendly thoughts in your mind. These kinds of thoughts lead to increased anxiety and worry.

Good Report and Praise

These two words are similar. Each one speaks of thinking thoughts that are positive. You can always find some bad news to think about and some bad news to discuss. Paul urges us to think of things that are of *good report.* Watch your thoughts. Don't fill your mind with rumors, gossip, and ugly things you hear about others. Think of something positive! You can always find something good to say about people.

I heard about one lady who was extremely positive. She always had something good to say about everyone and every situation. Two men were discussing her one day and decided to put her to the test. They just knew they had a way to make her say something negative.

When she arrived at church the following Sunday morning, one of the men said, "Miss Bertha, the devil sure is mean!" She replied, "Well, you have to admit that he is consistent. He really is consistent!"

I don't know if we have to be as positive as Miss Bertha, but speaking things that are of good report can help us find peace of mind in life. Please understand, I am not talking about "positive thinking" in the same way some promotional and motivational speakers talk about it. I am reminding you that God wants you to fill your mind with things that are of good report. Why? He wants you to do this because it aides in creating peace in your mind and rest in your heart. If you want to be free of anxiety, pray correctly and think rightly!

THINK ON THESE THINGS
The Lord implores us to *think on these things.* The Greek word used for our English word *think* is *logizomai.* This means to consider whether we are thinking correctly. Take an inventory of your thoughts. Do you think the way the Lord tells you to think? It just may be that your thinking process is leading you to a level of anxiety that is not good for you and makes you less effective in God's work.

DO QUICKLY
There is one more thing required to overcome anxiety. Paul tells his readers to *do* the things he has taught them to do and the things they have seen him do.

> The things which you learned and received and heard and saw in me, these do, and the God of peace will be with you.

Philippians 4:9

The word 'do' in this passage is written as a present, active, imperative verb. Paul is saying, "To have peace, you must do the right things and do them right now!" Paul taught and displayed a tranquil attitude in every situation. He did not change his demeanor or thought pattern with every crosswind of changing circumstance that blew across his life. He was always the same. That, after all, is a characteristic of Jesus—He is the same yesterday, today, and forever (Hebrews 13:8). One habit that assisted Paul in maintaining peace in his life was the way he viewed his responsibilities. Paul did what Paul was supposed to do and he is telling us to do likewise!

We are to *do* what we know we ought to *do*. To leave things undone, that we know should be done, creates an atmosphere of anxiety. This is especially true when it comes to obeying Christ. If it should be done, just *do it*!

This issue applies to every area of life, not just those things that we think of as being spiritual in nature. If you walk past a piece of furniture that needs to be dusted and you see it every day, just go ahead and dust it! The longer you look at and think about it, the more anxious you get. If the screen door needs to be repaired, just fix it. It is better than seeing it in disrepair and worrying about it. Just do it!

Of course, this principle applies even more importantly in our obedience to God's will. If you know you should witness to a neighbor, coworker, or relative, don't put it off. This will only make you more nervous. You know you should tithe, so just do it. Being obedient removes anxiety and creates a sense of rest and peace in the soul. Just do it!

Doing what you know you should do, when you become aware that you should do it, relieves more stress than you may realize. Just do it!

If you put these three things together, praying correctly, thinking rightly, and doing quickly what you know you should do, you will see that each part of the process serves the purpose of adding to your peace of mind. Practice these three things, and you will find rest in the Lord.

- Praying correctly is your upward or spiritual devotion
- Thinking rightly is your inward or personal devotion
- Doing quickly is your outward or practical devotion

Everything that happens in your life is upward, inward or outward. When each of these is in harmony, you will have the peace of God, and you will experience the God of peace fully in your life. Getting these three areas in balance will keep worry and anxiety from robbing you of the joy you are meant to have in your Christian life, and this balanced life will keep worry and anxiety from robbing you of the power and purpose that God has for you.

We are told in this passage of scripture that it is necessary for us to pray God's way, to think God's way, and to do the things we know God has told us to do. When we do these as we should, we have the promise that the *God of peace* will be with us. Yes, God is always with us as Christians; however, He is with us in a deeper and more peaceful way when we get our praying, thinking, and doing in line with His will.

Have you been nervous lately? Are you overanxious and worried? Perhaps you need to review the process you are going through in trying to deal with your problems. The simple secret to a more calm, restful, tranquil, composed, serene, and relaxed mind is to put the three things listed here into practice. You might want to reread this chapter a couple of times and start exercising a biblical prayer life, thinking process, and action plan. Exercise like an athlete. Take time to consider these three issues each day. Write them down and put them where you can see them often. Put the words from Philippians 4:13 on a card and place it on the mirror you use to comb your hair or apply your makeup. Repeat the words at least five days every morning and every night. Offer prayers to God that contain only praise and gratitude at least once each day. Think of something positive about people you know then sit down and write them a nice note letting them know of your thoughts. This kind of practice generates the habit of thinking things of good report. Each week, think of something you have been meaning to do but haven't done. Write it down and make sure you do it. It may be as simple as cleaning out a closet or calling an old friend. It may be volunteering to help your church in an upcoming event. It might be reaching out to someone with whom you have had a difference of opinion and renewing that friendship. Just do it. As you pray, think, and do things properly, a new divine peace will come into your life—the kind of rest God means for you to have as His child.

REST APPLICATION

In what Bible passage do we find Paul's description of overcoming worry and anxiety?

_____

Where was Paul when he wrote the words in Philippians that concern overcoming anxiety?

_____

Name at least three reasons why worry and anxiety is wrong:

_____

_____

_____

Praying right involves a critical element. What is it?

_____

Name at least three words that Paul used to describe the way we must think if we wish to truly rest in the Lord.

_____

_____

_____

Praying right involves our _____ devotion.
Thinking correctly involves our _____ devotion.
Doing immediately involves our _____ devotion.

WORSHIP

We worship God because He is worthy of our worship. Worship is both an expectation and a privilege for the child of God. Also, it is a private and a public issue. He calls us to worship, but if we belong to Him, we desire to worship in His presence. We must worship Him daily in the privacy of our places of residence, and we must worship Him in the House of the Lord with other believers.

When we worship the Lord properly, we discover that what begins as something we do for Him becomes something good for us. It lifts our eyes off this sin-cursed world and places them on the holiness and purity of God. We read in Isaiah 6:3 that there are those in heaven who worship the Lord incessantly, saying, "Holy, holy, holy is the Lord God Almighty!" Worship is the act of entering into the presence of God—Holy God! Those who abhor and dread worship will not be at home in heaven for those who are there worship Him continually and with abandon.

Worship helps us *minimize our problems and magnify our blessings*. It helps us realize that this world is not our home. It reduces the feeling that our *little lives* here are all that there is to living. Often, as we age, we look back more and more. We tend to talk about the "good old days." Yet when we were living those so-called good old days, we were looking forward to the "better future days." When we were children, we looked forward to being old enough to drive a car and being free of constant parental control. When we were teenagers, we couldn't wait to get out of school. Then we looked forward to marriage, to having children, and to having a home of our own. Then we started looking toward the day when we would not have to punch the clock at our job or profession; retirement sounded better all the time. Of course, some of us retired, found it wasn't what we thought it would be, and then went back to work or volunteered at the church or a charity a few days a week. The point is that we live most of our lifetime looking ahead. But senior adults can quickly come down with reverse imagination, otherwise known as the good old days syndrome. Worship helps us look up and look forward. It keeps our focus in the right direction.

We cannot experience all God has for us unless we intensify our worship. Mediocre worship leads to mediocrity in Christian living. We can't mumble through a song, nod off during prayer, and yawn through a sermon and call it worship. If we are looking backward momentarily to remember His blessings, forward with faith in His promises, and upward with a heart of love, we can live the lives God intends.

Let's use the example of automobile mirrors to understand how important it is to keep our major concentration on that which is above and that which is ahead rather on that which is behind. When a car is built, it has three rearview mirrors, and some of the new cars even have backup cameras. The mirrors and camera are not there so we can drive our cars around town in reverse gear but are installed so that we don't allow things behind us to cause accidents. Look how small those mirrors are when compared to the windshield on the automobile. The windshield is huge by comparison, and this is how it should be. It is clearly apparent that a driver of an automobile is to use the windshield far more than the rearview mirrors when driving the car. In life, it is just as important for us to learn that the rearview mirror of memory has its place, but looking back must not dominate our lives. We cannot move forward properly if we are always looking backward. We can learn from that which is behind us so that we don't repeat mistakes in our lives today, but life must be viewed through the windshield of the future. We do not need to have a life mirror that is the size of a windshield. To worship correctly, we simply must make the windshield, the future God is leading us toward, our paramount focus. Of course we remember the past, and we should, but spending too much time with what is behind us can prohibit us from moving onward and upward to what is before us!

Counting Your Blessings

One way that it is appropriate to encourage worship is to *glance* into the review mirror of life in order to count our blessings. We can't count our blessings without glancing back at how God has worked in our lives in the years gone by. Worship is encouraged and passionate when accompanied by remembrances of God's grace. Even when counting our blessings, we must be careful. It is possible to think of some wonderful experience we had in the past and then compare it to a hardship we are going through now and allow the contrast to lead us into depression and to rob us of our joy. Also, looking back can remind us of painful experiences, hurts, and hardships that deprive us of the blessings we have right now in the Lord. Remembering can be good, but it can also be unhealthy. We simply must make the past available in a small rearview mirror and look at the present and future through a wide, expansive windshield of faith.

Let's take a moment now to glance back and remember some things that can enhance our worship of the Lord. No matter what you have been through in your life or the sorrows you may be enduring right now, I want you to focus on *four blessings* every senior adult Christian has at this very moment.

The Blessing of Long Life

First, you have lived a long time, long enough to watch many years pass. You must remember that many people have not experienced this blessing. You should be grateful to God for the years He has given you. He brought you to this point because He has a purpose for you to be here. Someone once wrote, "Don't complain about old age. Remember that many people never got the chance to experience it." Each day is a blessing from God and means that God has you here for a reason. The spiritual song says, "He brought me from a mighty long way!"[7] Yes, He sure did, and He continues to lead us each day.

THE BLESSING OF SALVATION

Secondly, we are blessed because we are saved, and we have the promise that the Lord is with us every day. No matter how many loved ones who have gone before us in death or how many friends have passed away, we are never, ever really alone! One day we will have a homecoming day in heaven. We will rejoice with the saved that preceded us into God's presence. What a wonderful day that will be. If we remain here, He is with us; if we go home, we are with Him. Praise His name—we can't lose!

THE BLESSING OF DAILY NEEDS

Thirdly, though it may sound repetitive, we must be aware of the fact that God has new blessings for us *every day!* His Word tells us that God's mercies are new every morning! We are assured of new blessings each day that we live.

> Through the Lord 's mercies we are not consumed,
> Because His compassions fail not.
> They are new every morning;

Great is Your faithfulness.
"The Lord is my portion," says my soul,
"Therefore I hope in Him!"

Lamentations 3:22–24

Yes, great is the faithfulness of the Lord to His children. He never fails to show us His compassion, and His blessings are new each and every morning that we live. This is true even if we are unaware of those blessings. Take time each day to look for God's handiwork in your life. Every one of us is going through some hardship and trial, but we overcome the weight of these experiences by remembering each day the blessings He is providing. Don't concentrate on the burdens; place your attention on the blessings!

THE BLESSING OF BEING GOD'S SERVANTS

Fourthly, we have been given time to serve the Lord. This is a special blessing indeed. Serving the Lord is a joy to the Christian, and the joy of the Lord is our strength (Nehemiah 8:10). If we throw away the opportunities for service given to us each day of our lives, we are really tossing out occasions to be strengthened and blessed!

We could go on detailing our blessings from the Lord, but you get the point. We have been and are being blessed! Keep your focus on why God has you in the here and now, and apply your energies to serving and praising Him.

CONFIDENT IN YOUR SALVATION

Another blessing the Christian senior adult has is the assurance of salvation now and the promise of heaven in the future. The older we get, the closer we are to our homegoing. It provides great peace to know that we belong to Christ. Death has no more power over us than it had over Jesus. As long as He lives, we shall live, and He has already conquered death. A comedian once said, "I don't mind dying. I just don't want to be there when it happens!"[8] The great promise to the Christian is that the Lord will be there when death happens.

> Yea, though I walk through the valley of the
> shadow of death,
> I will fear no evil;
> For You are with me;
> Your rod and Your staff, they comfort me.
>
> Psalm 23:4

There is no mountain so high or valley so low that God is not present with those who know Him as Savior and Lord. God never promised believers that they would always dwell on mountaintops! Notice two precious promises from the Lord that prompt true worship.

First, we are going *through* the valley. We are not going to stay in the low places forever. We were never told that avoiding the valleys of life is possible, but we do have the promise that we are *going through the valleys*, and we will not dwell in these valleys unendingly. Also, being in a valley does not prohibit our ability to look upward to God. Many Christians have discovered God more intimately from a prison cell or a hospital room than they ever did from a mountaintop.

Secondly, we are told that He is *with us* when we are in the valley. Since we are walking *through* the valley and since the Lord is our Companion, we must count the journey as a blessing. We are saved and sure, and that comforts us in all situations. Worship Him today, even if you are struggling through some valley. He is still God. He will lead you onward and upward.

CONVINCED THAT THE LORD NEVER FAILS

Psalm 71 is sometimes referred to as *the old man's psalm.* It will serve us well when thinking on the subject of worship to take a look at this psalm and take note of the psalmist's words.

You could entitle this psalm "The Lord Never Fails." There is no doubt it was written by someone who knew the Lord and was older when he penned it. The psalmist who penned these words was going through a difficult time. He felt fear, abandonment, and could sense the hot breath of his enemies on his neck. But he continued to praise God. He would not forsake the privilege of worship, and it led him to share some victorious truths in the words he wrote.

This psalm can help us remember the Lord's great gift—our eternal security. Eternal life does not begin when we die; eternal life begins the moment a person places faith in Jesus as Lord and Savior. In essence, as pointed out earlier, every Christian is actually ageless!

Psalm 71:9, reads

> Do not cast me off in the time of old age;
> Do not forsake me when my strength fails.

Note the mention of old age in this psalm:

> O God, You have taught me from my youth;
> And to this day I declare Your wondrous works.
> Now also when I am old and grayheaded,
> O God, do not forsake me,
> Until I declare Your strength to this generation,
> Your power to everyone who is to come.
>
> Psalm 71:17–18

The man who penned these words was experiencing a strong sense of loneliness. He was concerned with being *forsaken*. However, the writer goes on to express his faith in God and shares some important things that we need to consider. These truths can help us worship today, even if problems and pains persist in our lives. When we consider these blessings, it will help increase energy in our worship, vitality in our service, and joy in our daily living.

OUR POSITION PSALM 71:1-8

The Christian is *in Christ*, and Christ is *in the Christian*. No matter what our circumstances appear to be in this present moment, we are secure and safe in Him. The psalmist used several illustrative ways to describe his secure position in the Lord as an aged believer.

A REFUGE

The psalmist stated that he had taken refuge in the Lord. The Hebrew word for *refuge* in this passage appears thirty-six times in the Old Testament. It means "to put one's trust in another." The psalmist made sure he added that he had taken refuge in the true God of heaven. The psalmist was not trusting in his wealth, position, or health. He knew that God never fails those who place their trust in Him for salvation, forgiveness, and blessings. He is our *refuge*, a place where we are safe *through* the storms of life. Worship Him today as your sure refuge!

A student at college asked his teacher, "Were you out in all that rain last night, professor?" The professor, being rather theoretically inclined, answered, "No, I was merely in the portion of the rain that descended in my immediate vicinity."

At times it may seem that the entire clouds of trouble have opened above your head and that all the showers of trouble have descended directly upon you—that not a single drop of the rain falling from the sky is missing you! But God knows where you are. You are safe in Him. In fact, God even uses the problems to increase our blessings!

The Scripture states the principle of blessing out of difficulty correctly:

> And we know that all things work together for good to those who love God, to those who are the called according to His purpose.
>
> Romans 8:28

Most people who quote Romans 8:28 leave out the words *we know*. To *know* that God can and will bring good out of every situation requires great faith. It requires faith in a loving, compassionate God who is in control. When we *know* that He is working in all of our circumstances, we can rest in the *refuge* He provides.

When we are confident of His love and protection, we can worship Him no matter what we are facing or enduring.

SAFE IN THE STORM

Imagine that a tornado warning has been issued in your area. You quickly look out the window of your home, and you actually see the huge funnel cloud coming in your direction. The wind is beginning to bend the trees, and the eerie sound created around the corners of your house generates a fearful sense of danger. Your first thought is to look for a place to hide. You might consider a closet, or perhaps lying in your tub, as a safe place to hide. Just as the storm is about to strike your home with winds up to two hundred miles per hour, you realize that you have no refuge. An awful feeling of dread ensues as the windows of your home are sucked outward and the roof begins to come apart above your head.

Change the imagined scenario and consider the difference it makes in the way you feel about this storm. The tornado is getting closer, but you have a deep and solid basement. You close the large basement door behind you and descend the steps down to a large room with concrete walls all around you. The storm passes by overhead, and you can hear the awful damage it is doing, but you are safe! You are cradled in the arms of your secure basement, and you pray for those who have no place to hide. And then you bow your head with tears and thank God that you are safe!

So let the storm clouds rage high,
The dark clouds rise,
They don't bother me;
For I'm sheltered in the arms of God.
He walks with me,
And naught of earth shall harm me,
For I'm sheltered in the arms of God.[9]

Worship involves being aware of the *refuge* we have in Christ. His safe and strong refuge, when fully realized, causes you to rejoice and to praise Him. Indeed, He holds us in His hand. Yes, the storms of life pound all around us and sometimes seem to come straight at us, but Jesus is our shelter in the storms of life and in the great storm of death. The songwriter penned, "Keep me safe till the storm passes by."[10] You can be sure that He will keep those safe who trust Him throughout every storm and until the final storm has passed them by.

No Posse Is Pursuing Us

When I was a boy growing up in North Carolina, my friends and I went to the movie theater almost every Saturday. In those days the movies were innocuous, and our parents didn't have to worry about us seeing things we shouldn't see or hearing things we shouldn't hear. Almost every week, a Western movie was the feature. Often, the guys wearing the black hats and running from the law would find a hideout—a place to conceal themselves from the Texas Rangers or the posse following them in rapid pursuit. But the hideout never worked. The good guys always found the crooks and took them in, or shot them with their six-shooters.

Have you ever thought of yourself as a crook? Well, to a certain extent, that is what you and I are. We have all sinned against a holy and righteous God (Romans 3:23). We are the bad guys, and there is nowhere to hide from God. But instead of coming to search for us so that He might punish us, the Lord sought us out that He might save us. Just read Luke 15, and you will see the picture of the searching shepherd looking for the lost sheep. When the Lord finds us, and we accept His grace, He provides a refuge from all the enemies of our souls. Jesus came after us not to punish us, but to give us security and peace.

The only place where it is safe to hide in this world is in the Lord. He is a refuge in a dangerous land. He covers us, keeps us, and protects us through His power, grace, and love. He will never let anyone take us out of His hand (John 10:28–29)! There is no attack, no storm, and no enemy that can remove us from God's love found in Christ (Romans 8:31–39). Indeed, if God is for us, who can be against us? This thought alone can trigger a burst of praise from the child of God.

A RESCUE
Another idea of safety presented in Psalm 71 is that of a rescue. The word *deliver* in this passage means "to rescue." The psalmist realized that only the Lord could deliver him.

THE REARVIEW MIRROR OF PRAISE
Let's go back for a moment and think of the rearview mirror analogy. A proper use of the rearview mirror in life is to think of the times that God has rescued us—

has delivered us—out of circumstances that seemed impossible at the time. We ought to glance back into the past and recall God's goodness to us so we can move forward without fear into the unknown future. We glance at the past, see how God has blessed us, and then we turn our attention to the glorious future He has for us! When Jesus called His disciples, He said, "Come, follow me." That is what He still does each day. We can't follow that which we cannot see. Keep your eyes on Him. Worship Him. Make it a daily practice to do so.

Let's go back for a moment to the Western movie idea I mentioned earlier. Almost every time I saw one of those old Western movies, a pretty young lady would be in danger from a mustachioed, beady-eyed, mean, dangerous man. Sometimes the movie would portray the unfortunate woman strapped to a railroad track or tied up with ropes in a cabin. At the last minute, when all hope appeared to be lost, she would be rescued by some daring, muscular, good-looking guy. Even though I knew the rescue was going to happen, I breathed a little easier once she was safe. Oh, how wonderful that Jesus cut the ropes holding us and rescued us from sin's grip and Satan's schemes. He literally snatched us from death! Having done this for us through His Son, He will not withhold any good thing from us (Romans 8:32).

RESCUED AND REJOICING

So it is a good thing to use the rearview mirror to recall the blessings God has bestowed upon us. It helps us to have a heart of worship. If we think only upon the problems we are experiencing at the moment, it hinders our proper worship of the Lord. We need to count our blessings so we can worship the Lord with a heart of gratitude. Why not stop right now and think of five wonderful things the Lord has done for you that deserve your worship today? Just stop right now, put this book down, and worship Him in a spirit of gratitude and joy. Tell Him how thankful you are that He has been with you and brought you through all the many trials and hardships you have endured. Thank Him for the doors He has opened for you, and perhaps you can praise Him right now for a few doors He has closed as well. There are times when God says no to our prayers, and it is only much later that we realize God knew best. Worship is enhanced when we recall that God has been good to us. Take a moment and write down some wonderful things God has done for you. Then stop and praise Him! Worship Him! Love Him!

A RIGHTEOUSNESS

In addition to the image of a refuge and a rescue, we see in this psalm the *righteousness of God imparted to those who trust Him*. The word *righteousness* speaks of purity and holiness. I am not just saved from my sins; I am made like Jesus in purity and holiness. The unrighteous are made righteous when they turn from their sins and place faith in Christ. Just think of what this means:

- I am as spotless as God says I am.
- I am as safe as God says I am.
- I am as saved as God says I am.

Be thankful each day for the blessing of being righteous in Christ. But just in case someone reads this who thinks he or she is righteous due to his or her own good deeds, read carefully the following passage from Isaiah:

> But we are all like an unclean thing,
> And all our righteousnesses are like filthy rags;
> We all fade as a leaf,
> And our iniquities, like the wind,
> Have taken us away.
>
> Isaiah 64:6

The Bible tells us that aside from the grace of God, even our good works are like filthy rags. To understand this, imagine a doctor doing surgery. The doctor is well trained, and he has every good intention while doing the surgery. He is truly trying to do the right thing, but he has unseen germs on his hands. During the surgery, he passes those germs on to his patient. The doctor is practicing good works, but he is contaminated. That is the way our works and deeds are without Christ in our lives. And there is no water or soap to wash away the pollution of the human soul. Only the sacrifice of Jesus, His shed blood at Calvary, can make a person clean— righteous. He is the only cure for unrighteousness. But once we are saved and cleansed through His sacrifice at Calvary, we have His righteousness imputed (given) to us. We are pure in Him. We do not serve Him in order to obtain righteousness; we serve Him because He has made us righteous through His Son. Now that is something to be thankful for today and every day!

We are thinking just now concerning the way we should be enjoying the blessings we already have and the fact that those blessings should lead us to be a worshipping people. When counting our blessings, it is easy for us to think of things like food, clothes, and shelter, and we should be thankful for those things, but we need to express our gratitude first and foremost for provisions God has given us that we cannot lose. Begin each day in gratitude for His grace, love, and salvation! Keep in mind that His righteousness is what we needed most, something we could never provide for ourselves, and something He has given us that will never be taken away from us!

A ROCK

Another word that the Psalmist used to describe His position in the Lord in Psalm 71 is the word *rock*. In the Holy Land, rocks are prevalent, and they are appreciated. In Israel, the Holy Land, most homes are built out of rocks and stones. Those homes are strong and secure. When building those homes, they seek to erect them on strong, solid foundations. When hard rains come and the winds blow, the homes made of rock and established on rock can withstand the forces of nature exerted upon them. But houses built on sand can be swept away. Tents that are pitched in low areas are often carried away in a storm or flood. But anything attached to a rock is steadfast and immoveable! The psalmist pictures God as the great Rock of Ages on which we are established and secure. God never changes; He is like a mighty rock! The songwriter penned, "On

Christ the solid rock I stand, all other ground is sinking sand, all other ground is sinking sand."[11]

Jesus spoke about this in Matthew 7:24–26. He pointed out clearly that a life established on the sands of philosophy or false religion will be swept away in the storm that is coming; however, the life founded upon the Solid Rock is immovable. Jesus is that Rock, and one resting upon Him cannot be moved. No storm can approach that is able to remove the person who has taken shelter upon the Rock of Ages!

A man tumbled from a ship near the shore in a terrible storm many years ago. People on the shoreline knew he was out there in the water but could not see him, and thus a rescue was impossible. They stood helpless and thought for sure that he had drowned. The next morning, they saw him not far from the shore clinging to a rock. Quickly they launched a small boat and brought him ashore. He was cold, wet, and trembling when they laid him out on the sand and wrapped him in some blankets. One man said to him, "I know you must have been terribly frightened out there during the night." The rescued man said, "Not really. Though the wind and rain was horrible, the rock didn't move!"[12]

We are settled on the *Rock* that will not move. He is our safe place in a world of storms and rainy days. We need only keep our thoughts on the blessing of the Rock rather than concentrating on the storms—our aches, pains, sorrows, and troubles. When we remember that we are established forever on the Rock, we can worship with a heart full of joy and love.

A RULER

The psalmist also speaks in Psalm 71 of the Lord as Sovereign—the One who reigns and rules. He is King of kings and Lord of lords. He is supreme above all authorities. Even though we cannot always see the King, we can know that He is working to bring about what is best for us and that which will bring Him glory. He is crowned with glory, and no one can take His throne. He will never be unseated or usurped by another, and He will never abrogate His throne or resign His position. World leaders come and go, but the King of kings still reigns. You are part of His family, a royal priesthood.

> But you are a chosen generation, a royal priesthood, a holy nation, His own special people, that you may proclaim the praises of Him who called you out of darkness into His marvelous light; who once were not a people but are now the people of God, who had not obtained mercy but now have obtained mercy.
>
> 1 Peter 2:1–9

Note that you and I are to *proclaim the praises of Him.* We are to be a worshipping people, both in public and private. Rejoice in your place in God's family, and treat others in the family as children of the King!

Yes, He is the God of the past, but He is also the Lord of the present and future. He has not changed. Hebrews 13:8 states this clearly: "Jesus Christ is the same yesterday, today, and forever."

So you can see from these images that the ground of your salvation is secure today and will be secure tomorrow! Each example the psalmist used revealed the nature of God, but they also revealed a series of reasons that the psalmist was rejoicing. These images, when considered seriously, can help us to worship God more fully. The Lord, who saved us through great personal sacrifice, will never leave us, never forsake us, and never allow us to fall. Rejoice! Worship! You will *feel* better, *live* better, and *look* better each day as you worship Him fully and faithfully.

OUR PLEA – PSALM 71:6-13

The psalmist did not stop at the point of rejoicing. He moved on to reveal how he prayed in difficult times. The psalmist cried out to God as recorded in Psalm 71:6–13. Thorny problems, demanding situations, and tough times have always been a part of life, even for God's people; in fact, arduous challenges have at times especially confronted God's people. Calling upon God to help us is also a part of worship. I assure you that God is more concerned with you staying in contact with Him than He is with you getting everything you pray for. Prayer is not just a time for us to treat God like a holy bellhop or glorified Santa Claus. He is not just sitting around waiting for us to tell Him what we need! He is God. He wants us to talk to Him and desires that we stay in contact with Him. Praying is part of that process. When we worship Him in prayer as we should, the Spirit of God helps in our praying. The Spirit of God in us makes pleas to the Father that we are not even aware of when we are praying.

> Likewise the Spirit also helps in our weaknesses. For we do not know what we should pray for as we ought, but the Spirit Himself makes intercession for us with groanings which cannot be uttered. Now He who searches the hearts knows what the mind of the Spirit is, because He makes intercession for the saints according to the will of God.
>
> Romans 8:26–27

Praying accomplishes more than we realize. When we worship God with sincere prayer, He helps us in ways that go beyond mere words. You may feel your prayers are ineffective and that you lack the ability to offer lovely prayers like those you hear other people pray. Dear Christian, never make light of your prayers. God knows your heart and considers that far more important than your elocution or vocabulary when he hears you praying.

As the psalmist prayed, he revealed some areas of concern that affect most of us as senior adult Christians.

THE FEAR HE FELT

Psalm 71 reveals that the writer was dealing with *fear*. As we grow older, we tend to experience more fear. We can begin to feel that we are being cast away by family, society, and even by the Lord. We feel vulnerable as we age. Perhaps the psalmist was feeling a sense of being jettisoned or discarded because he was going through great difficulties and he did not have the strength of his youth to aid him in overcoming the strain of enduring those hardships. He prayed for God not to cast him away.

Old age has its own set of fears. The fear of illness, the fear of losing mental capacities, and the fear of loneliness can be a bit overwhelming. It is not unnatural to experience these fears, but we can have victory over them through the Lord.

THE FOES HE FACED

The psalmist who penned Psalm 71 indicated that he was being persecuted by enemies. I don't know what enemies you may be facing, but God is bigger than your enemies. There is no enemy greater than the friend who is closer than a brother. John wrote, "You are of God, little children, and have overcome them, because He who is in you is greater than he who is in the world (1 John 4:4)."

I understand that we each face different levels of stress in life. Actually, my problems always seem more severe than those someone else is facing. Don't you feel the same way about your problems? I remember a man saying to me, "I am having a small cancer removed from my face. I don't care how small it is, it is a major surgery when a doctor puts a scalpel in his hand and approaches my body!" So whatever problems we face, they are major when they are personal. But we can find peace in the promises, power, and presence of the Lord. True worship connects us to Him.

You recall, I am sure, that night mentioned in the New Testament when Jesus came walking on the water to His disciples who were in a boat in the midst of a storm. Peter wanted to go to the Lord by walking on the water. Note what happened to Peter once he stepped out of the boat:

> And Peter answered Him and said, "Lord, if it is You, command me to come to You on the water."
>
> So He said, "Come." And when Peter had come down out of the boat, he walked on the water to go to Jesus. But when he saw that the wind was boisterous, he was afraid; and beginning to sink he cried out, saying, "Lord, save me!"
>
> And immediately Jesus stretched out His hand and caught him, and said to him, "O you of little faith, why did you doubt?"
>
> Matthew 14:28–31

Peter stepped out of the boat and began to walk on the water. Then note specifically what happened to him. "But when he saw that the wind was boisterous, he was afraid; and beginning to sink he cried out, saying, 'Lord, save me.'" Peter took his eyes off the Lord and placed them on the waves. The moment he looked away from Jesus, he became frightened. Fear is often the result of concentrating on the windy problems blowing across our path rather than fixing our eyes on the Lord who has authority over the wind! Worship helps us keep our attention on Him. When we fix our hearts upon Him in worship, every problem seems smaller and every difficulty more manageable.

Keep your eyes on Christ! You cannot help but glance at your problems, the things you consider enemies, but you and I need to keep our attention fixed on the Lord. Paul wrote in Colossians 3:2, "Set your mind on things above, not on things on the earth." It was wise advice when he wrote it, and it is God's Word to us today!

David spoke of God leading him in a precious psalm:

> The Lord is my shepherd
> I shall not want.
> He makes me to lie down in green pastures;
> He leads me beside the still waters.
> He restores my soul;
> He leads me in the paths of righteousness
> For His name's sake.
>
> Psalm 23:1–3

"He leads me" is repeated twice in these three verses, and it is implied in verse 1 where David speaks of the Lord as "*my Shepherd*." Don't concentrate on your enemies or problems; keep your eyes on the Shepherd, the Leader. The songwriter penned,

> He leadeth me, O blessed thought!
> O words with heav'nly comfort fraught!
> Whate'er I do, where'er I be
> Still 'tis God's hand that leadeth me.
> He leadeth me, He leadeth me,
> By His own hand He leadeth me;
> His faithful foll'wer I would be,
> For by His hand He leadeth me.[13]

Yes, He leads those who are following Him. He cannot lead you where you will not follow. Worship is an act of saying, "Lord, I have my eyes fixed upon you.

I will go where you lead me. I trust you. I worship you. I adore you. Lead on, great God and King!"

THE FAITH HE FOCUSED

In Psalm 71, the psalmist focused his faith upon God. He knew the Lord personally and spoke of Him as "my God." He called on God to be near Him, ("Be not far from me"), and he fixed his faith upon the Lord.

As we grow older, we face issues peculiar to our age. New fears and foes can seem to encircle us. We gain victory over them by focusing our faith in the Lord. John wrote, "For whatever is born of God overcomes the world. And this is the victory that has overcome the world—our faith" (1 John 5:4).

Faith is a Bible word that is often thrown around rather loosely. We can talk about it without having the slightest idea of its meaning. We can be guilty of using *churchy words* that sound good but don't mean much to us because we don't really know how to apply them in real-life situations. The Bible says our victory comes through faith, but how does faith give us victory? Faith is not the act of thinking positive thoughts, nor is it the act of talking ourselves into believing that things will work out the way we want them to. Faith is the act of connecting our hearts and minds to God.

Let's think for a moment about how faith works by looking at a concrete biblical example of what the word 'faith' really means. In Ephesians 2:8, we read, "For by grace you have been saved through faith, and that not of yourselves; it is the gift of God." We know this verse is one that speaks of salvation through Christ alone, but there is something else in this verse that is very important and can be easily overlooked. Note that Paul used the word *through* when speaking of faith. Grace comes to us *through* faith. In other words, *faith is a conduit through which the blessing of grace is passed to us.*

Faith is a conduit. Perhaps you have seen videos of tanker planes fueling fighter jets while both are in flight. The tanker plane feeds a tube-like device down to a fighter jet flying below it. The fighter jet gets into the right position, and the tube from the tanker plane is connected to the fighter jet. Then the jet fuel is moved from the tanker plane into the fighter jet. It is an amazing exploit to watch. Think of faith as an invisible tube by which you connect to God's supply of blessings for your life. When we believe God—really believe His promises, His love, and His power—we get into a position for Him to deliver resources from His limitless supply into our limited lives. Faith connects us to Him, and from Him the blessings pass to us. Without faith, we cannot be connected to God and to His blessings.

It is important that we do not misunderstand this analogy. A Christian is always connected to God. Faith was required for us to trust Him for salvation in the first place. We can't lose our salvation, and we never lose connection to Him once we are saved, but there is more to faith than mere saving faith. It is continuing faith in God that activates His power in our personal situations.

Let's think of another example of faith at work in the Christian's life. A home has a connection to electric power. The power is produced somewhere else and is delivered to the home through a wiring system, a connection from the supply to the need. However, the power is not activated unless the home owner is willing to trust that the supply is available and is willing to flip the switch to turn on the lights in the home. Most of us have so much faith in the power company that we flip the switch to turn on the lights in our homes without a second thought. God has the power for our needs and circumstances, and every Christian is connected to Him through Christ; however, His power is not released in full measure unless we are willing to *flip* the switch of faith! For the Christian, the power of God is already connected, but the Christian can be guilty of not appropriating it. Faith is the channel by which the blessings are triggered.

We overcome the enemy, not by our own strength, but by the strength of the Lord. Keep your focus on God and not on your fears and foes. By doing so, you will position yourself in the arena of faith. From that position, you will find God refueling you with His energy, peace, power, wisdom, strength, love, and grace. By focusing on God's power and not your own weaknesses, you will discover the flow of His energy into your situation. All you need, He has. All you believe Him for, He can supply. His tank never runs empty. His power plant never shuts down. Worshipping regularly and genuinely aides us in connecting to the Lord by faith. Thus, worship is a key to victory in our Christian living.

Faith is not magic. Faith is not magic. We do not have faith in faith; we have faith in God. Hebrews 11:6 states, "But without faith it is impossible to please

Him, for he who comes to God must believe that He is, and that He is a rewarder of those who diligently seek Him." Note, we are not seeking the blessings; we are seeking the Blesser! We are not just trying to connect to the supply; we are seeking to connect to the Supplier! In essence, we are seeking to connect fully with Him, not just with the supply He can provide for us. Faith in God pleases Him, and the results of our faith will please us!

We actually worship God in faith. We have faith that we are in His presence. We have faith that He has blessed us and that our good fortune in life has not simply been coincidence. We have faith that He will supply our need. We have faith that He will enable us to serve and be useful in His kingdom. People who are weak in faith are also weak in worship, and people who are weak in worship are weak in almost every other area of Christian living. The greater our faith, the more powerful our worship; and the more powerful our worship, the greater our faith! One builds upon the other. When practiced properly, faith and worship becomes a perpetual engine of spiritual strength.

As we age, our bodies grow weaker and our strength ebbs, but age and time need not weaken our faith or worship. Keep your focus on Him and your faith in Him in every situation.

So we have learned that we are secure in Christ, and we know that His grace supplies all we need as we keep our faith in Him.

Our Praise (Psalm 71:14–24). Praise is important, and we note that the psalmist expressed jubilant praise to God. Praise is evidence that we know Him and trust Him. It is an act of expressing gratitude for who God is, what He has done, and what He has promised to do.

One cannot truly praise God and complain at the same time. We cannot whine and worship simultaneously. In Psalm 71, the writer as facing problems, but he was focused on praising God!

First, we have praise *for* the Lord. In Psalm 71, the psalmist commits to *make known* the greatness of God and the great deeds God has performed. The psalmist has praise for the Lord that he intends for other people to know and hear. We do this when we praise Him in public worship and when we extol Him in personal witnessing.

It is interesting to note how much time we spend using negative words and speaking of negative things. Robert Schrauf, associate professor of Applied Linguistics and an anthropologist at Penn State University, made a study of the positive and negative words in the human language. He found that fifty percent of all our words are negative while thirty percent are positive and twenty percent are neutral. Schrauf wrote, "Studies of 37 different languages turned up seven words that have very similar meanings. They are joy, fear, anger, sadness, disgust, shame and guilt. Seven words, and only one positive. Isn't that awesome?"[14]

What Schrauf discovered is that people, no matter their language or geographical location, are prone to complain more than they are to praise. As senior adult Christians, we should be different. We have the Spirit of God dwelling in our lives. We should be lifting up praises to the Lord. We should make known through worship and praise all the wonderful things He is doing and has done for us. When we are inclined to complain, whine, or moan, we need to recall the wonders God has shown us in His Word and the wonders God He has revealed to us in daily living. No Christian is without some blessing for which he or she can give public praise! When you worship the Lord as you should, you compel others to join in the praise.

I am convinced that many more people would come to the Lord if Christians, especially senior adult Christians, would just be more positive and open about how good God has been and how wonderful God is in their lives. It may be true that people like bad news, but people are never drawn to the Lord by grumbling, griping, complaining, whining believers. People need the Lord, and they are drawn to Him when they hear how wonderful life is for those who know Him. Take time each day to consider how often you mention the goodness of God to others.

Secondly, we will have praise *with* the Lord in His presence one day. In Psalm 71:19–21, we have a record of the faith of the psalmist that God will raise him up from the earth; he believes that God will one day resurrect his body! He knows that the day will come when he will actually praise the Lord *in person*.

I have always been amazed by the ads that appear for entertainers, especially those that have bold letters across a poster that reads "Live and in Person." When reading a poster like that, I have always been inclined to say "Well, thank goodness he is not appearing *dead and in person!*"

One day every saved person will meet Jesus "live and in person"! Glory! What a day that will be when we bow at His feet and give Him the glory due His name—in person! Of course, He is alive now and forevermore, but what a day that will be when we see Him face-to-face. Since we are going to be with Him one day in the future, we should be practicing our praise in the here and now! We can live in a state of joy because this world—so filled with sadness, pain, and death—is not our final home. As wonderful as life is, it is filled with sorrows, hurts, pain, and suffering; after all, it is a fallen world. Job 14:1 reads,

> "Man *who is* born of woman
> Is of few days and full of trouble."

But we are going to a new home. We are pilgrims here. Rejoice in the promise of the home prepared for you by Christ where we will be with Him where He is!

> In My Father's house are many mansions; if it were not so, I would have told you. I go to prepare a place for you. And if I go and prepare a place for you, I will come again and receive you to Myself; that where I am, there you may be also.
>
> John 14:2–3

If you do not have assurance that you have placed your faith in Christ, do it now. Simply admit that you are a sinner and that your sin has separated you from God. Believe that Jesus was God's Son and that he died on the cross to remove your sins. Believe that God raised Him from the dead and that He is Lord! Confess Him as your personal Savior and Lord right now. If you are making this decision for the first time, speak to the person leading your Bible study about your decision, or call a local pastor and explain your commitment to Christ. These leaders can help you follow Christ more fully.

Of course, most of you reading this book made a commitment to Christ long ago. Those of us who have trusted Jesus need to be the ones praising Him and making Him known to others. We should publicly make known His goodness and graciousness toward us.

Thirdly, we consider praise *to* the Lord. Yes, one day we will praise Him in person, but it is also true that we must direct our *praise to the Lord* now. Praise for the Lord is telling others what He has done, but Praise to the Lord is reminding the Lord of what He has done. The last four verses of Psalm 71 speak of praise *to* the Lord. Yes, we will sing to Him in heaven, which is clearly recorded in the book of Revelation, but we are called upon to sing to Him *now*.

> I will sing to the Lord as long as I live;
> I will sing praise to my God while I have my being.
>
> Psalm 104:33

Like the psalmist, we should be singing to the Lord as long as we live in this world. In order to sing praises to the Lord daily, we have to concentrate upon Him and not our circumstances. It is easy to sing praises when everything is going our way, but we must praise Him in every situation. Paul wrote in Philippians 4:4, "Rejoice in the Lord always. Again I will say, Rejoice!" The most important word in that text is the word *always*. When Paul wrote Philippians 4:4, he was in a Roman prison. He took the idea of praising the Lord *always* seriously and personally. Paul praised the Lord even in the worst of circumstances. Our predicaments must never prohibit our praises!

I lived and pastored in the mountains early in my ministerial life. An elderly woman who lived there, she was in her nineties at the time, told me the following story that had been handed down in mountain lore. It seems a man named Carl was leaning against a tree by the side of the road one day with an ax nearby. Another man came walking down the road and stopped to speak. "Carl, what are doing leaning against that tree?" Carl answered, "I'm waiting to work up a sweat, and once I do, I going to chop up some wood for my fireplace." The other man said, "Carl, if you will start chopping, the sweat will appear, but if you keep waiting, you might freeze to death this winter."

The point is well taken. If you and I wait for everything to be perfect before we start worshipping God, we are not likely to ever get started. If, however, we start praising Him, we will discover the warmth of the joy that comes from it.

Like Paul, the psalmist said that he had a song of praise to the Lord and he was going to sing it, notwithstanding the fact that he was surrounded by enemies and hardships! He actually gave us the themes for the three verses of his praise song in the later part of this psalm:

- Theme one: for the *faithfulness of God* – Psalm 71:22
- Theme two: for the *graciousness of God* – Psalm 71:23
- Theme three: for the *righteousness of God* – Psalm 71:24

As a Christian, you have a song. *You and I are to sing the blessings; we are not supposed to be singing the blues*! Let us enjoy the blessings God has given us and the ones He has promised us. Through praise and worship to Him, we let others know of His wonderful blessings and position ourselves to be a blessing to others!

We need to take moment to consider a *praise problem* that has arisen in the church in recent years. One thing that has taken place in the church in recent times is the special praise time in worship services. Many churches now have a block of time in the worship service that is called praise time. Young Christians are especially attracted to this kind of worship activity. Some senior adults find this practice a bit disconcerting since many of them grew up with a worship surrounded with a quiet reverence for God. We should not despise the new music and practice of praise in worship. It may seem strange and different to us, but worship styles change through the years.

Consider the way God's people worshipped in the time of David. We discover that worshippers were very expressive as they praised the Lord. They played instruments, fell down before God on their faces, raised their hands, and shouted. In fact, in some of David's psalms, he called upon worshippers to shout to the Lord.

At other times in history, worship was more subdued. Worship styles are constantly shifting through the years. In our modern world, we can find churches that are very reverent and sedate in worship. On the other hand, there are modern churches that have music in worship that resembles a rock concert. And then of course, one can find churches with styles of music and praise in between the two extremes.

No one should feel that it is necessary to participate in any behavior during worship that is not spontaneously activated by the Spirit of God; at the same time, we must not begrudge others the opportunity to express themselves in worship as long as their practice is not drawing attention to themselves or found to be in violation of Scripture. The point here is that we must express ourselves sincerely in worship. We need to sing to the Lord and open our hearts to Him. It is simply unacceptable to go through public or private worship in a mechanical or obligatory fashion. Our hearts must be activated when we are worshipping the Lord!

> Make a joyful shout to the Lord , all you lands!
> Serve the Lord with gladness;
> Come before His presence with singing.
> Know that the Lord , He is God;

It is He who has made us, and not we ourselves;
We are His people and the sheep of His pasture.
Enter into His gates with thanksgiving,
And into His courts with praise.
Be thankful to Him, and bless His name.
For the Lord is good;
His mercy is everlasting,
And His truth endures to all generations.

Psalm 100

We are told in this psalm to make a *joyful shout* to the Lord. We are to *enter* the place of worship with *gladness*. We need to prepare our hearts for worship and arrive ready to praise God. No one should ever be able to describe us as the 'frozen chosen,' and to avoid this requires warming up in private the worship you plan to give Him in public. The reason many people have so little joy in public worship services is because they have spent so little time worshipping Him in private! As senior adults, let us be the ones who exemplify what it means to come ready to give praise to the Lord. We cannot enter His courts with thanksgiving unless we spend some time praising Him in our daily lives. Publically and privately, praise should be our practice.

James McGranahan (1840–1907) penned these words.

Our Lord is now rejected,
And by the world disowned,
By the many still neglected,
And by the few enthroned;
But soon He'll come in glory!
The hour is drawing nigh,
For the crowning day is coming

By-and-by.[15]

Let us be among those who enthrone the Lord in our hearts, proclaim Him in our witness, praise Him in our worship, exalt Him in our behavior, and keep looking for His coming. Lift up your head, your redemption is near!

If you want your senior years to be fulfilling, worship the Lord with all your heart. Take time to worship Him daily. Come ready to worship Him in God's house on the Lord's Day. You have reason to worship Him, so do it!

WORSHIP APPLICATION

Why do we worship God as senior adult believers?

_____

Has looking in the rearview mirror ever been a negative thing for you? In what way?

_____

Name four things you can be thankful for *right now* in your life as a senior Christian.

1. _____

2. _____

3. _____

4. _____

In Psalm 71, the psalmist mentions five ways that we are secure in the Lord. See if you can write down at least three of them and add a short sentence stating what each one means to you:

1. _____

2. _____

3. _____

We all face certain *fears*, and we likely feel that we have some *foes* in our lives. What is the great conduit that connects us to God so we can have victory in these issues? (If you can't remember, read Hebrews 11:6.)

_____

Complete the following sentence:

We cannot *praise* God and _____ at the same time.

Check the correct sentence below:

_____ Most words that humans speak of positive.

_____ Most words that humans speak are negative.

Is the following sentence true or false? Is it the job of the music minister and pastor to get me excited about worshipping God when I am in church each week?

_____ True

_____ False

SUFFER

We all try to avoid suffering whenever possible, and most of the time that is the right thing to do, but suffering is a part of life and cannot be totally circumvented. A member of a church I was pastoring was told that he had an aneurism in his aorta. I went to visit him in the hospital, and he shared that they were going to do surgery on him the next day. All of us at the church lovingly called him Pop. I said, "Pop, I'm sure you're going to be just fine." Pop replied, "Preacher, you don't understand, pain hurts me." With a smile, I said, "Pop, that's why they call it pain. Pain hurts everybody." We laughed about that later, but the point must be made that none of us like to endure pain and suffering.

Suffering, on the other hand, is sometimes the correct thing to embrace. Soldiers have willingly suffered to protect our country. Athletes suffer during sports events in order to play at their best, often playing with bruises, cuts, and even cracked bones. Mothers suffer to bring their children into the world. Jesus willingly suffered so that you and I might be forgiven and have eternal life. Suffering is not enjoyable, but it is often necessary in order to make progress, help others, and participate fully in life.

It seems like a strange thing to say, but the longer we live, the more we suffer. Senior adults are much more likely to know the experience of suffering than those who are young. A seventeen-year-old may have suffered the pain of not getting the toy he wanted as a child, or the heartbreak of unsuccessful puppy love, or perhaps the agony of seeing his high school team lose a game in the state championship, but he is unlikely to have experienced the manifold nature of suffering that a person eighty years of age has seen. The longer our days on earth, the greater the possibility of enlarged suffering. This is not to say that young people do not suffer; many of them do suffer greatly. However, the longer we live, the more likely we are to come face-to-face with increased sorrow, pain, disappointment, loneliness, and grief. If we do not guard against it, we can become bitter as we grow older simply because we have faced increased suffering. Learning to suffer gracefully is an important aspect of the Christian life.

It has been my experience to discover God's presence and grace more fully in suffering than in pleasure, though I would have opted for pleasure if the choice were mine. Actually, *hardships can impede us or improve us.* Problems can make us *bitter or they can make us better.* Our attitudes and actions during suffering determine whether the suffering brings about positive or negative results. If we trust God through adversity, we can encounter Him in new and deeper ways. Suffering has a way of causing us to appreciate our blessings more fully and to appropriate God's comfort more completely. If we allow suffering to make us cynical or resentful, we will harm ourselves, hinder our opportunities for knowing God more personally, and decrease the prospect of our making Him known to others.

THE LEGACY ENHANCED
THROUGH SUFFERING

Few great writers, poets, musicians, or ministers have reached the pinnacle of success without knowing pain and suffering. Dr. George W. Truett was the pastor of First Baptist Church in Dallas, Texas, for many years. He was a wonderfully gifted preacher. At some point in his ministerial life, he went hunting, and on that occasion Dr. Truett accidentally shot and killed one of his best friends. Dr. Truett was devastated by the accident and seriously considered leaving the ministry. His depression and distress was so deep that he was not sure he could return to the pulpit. He slowly recovered from the shock of that experience, and the Lord led him to continue preaching the Gospel. It was said by those who knew him before and after the accident that Dr. Truett portrayed a more profound pathos in his voice and demeanor after he had spent some time in the scalding caldron of suffering. He was a good preacher before the accident, but he was a great and mighty preacher afterward.

When suffering is embraced with faith in God, it has a way of reaching down into the deepest part of our souls and bringing God's grace to the surface. Such suffering grounds us and places us on a foundation that is solid and sure.

One of the great preachers in Scotland and England in the twentieth century was James S. Stewart. He was known as a preacher of unusual ability. He served for a time as chaplain to the Queen of Scotland. In his book *The Strong Name*, Dr. Stewart wrote three chapters on "God and the Fact of Suffering."[16] He points out that those who doubt God's existence because of the suffering they see in the world are seldom the ones doing the suffering. They are what Stewart called observers of suffering and not necessarily the participants in it. In fact, the greatest sufferers in the Bible had the greatest faith. We hear some preachers today claiming that true faith in God leads one above the swirling waters of sorrow; however, that is not what we find when we read the Bible.

In his book *Surprised By Suffering: The Role of Pain and Death in the Christian Life*, R. C. Sproul writes:

> Suffering is one of the most significant challenges to any believer's faith. When pain, grief, persecution or other forms of suffering strike, we find ourselves caught off guard, confused and full of questions. Suffering can strain faith to the limits.[17]

Sproul is correct. Suffering can twist one's mind and heart into knots. Randy Alcorn writes, "Jonie Eareckson Tada, reflecting on forty years in a wheelchair, told me, 'I've learned that suffering is messier than I first thought.'"[18] All of us learn this fact as we suffer. Suffering has been a part of life for all believers to one extent or another. We need to continue throughout our lives learning how to endure hardship and grow through it. It is useless to attempt to understand suffering; it is beyond our ability and intellect to explain the fact of suffering and reason for all of it. We can, however, suffer with faith, and we can know that we are bound for a place where we are promised that no suffering will occur.

WHAT DOES THE BIBLE SAY ABOUT SUFFERING?

In Hebrews 11, we read about those who had great faith. As the chapter comes to a close, we discover these words:

> Others were tortured, not accepting deliverance, that they might obtain a better resurrection. Still others had trial of mockings and scourgings, yes, and of chains and imprisonment. They were stoned, they were sawn in two, were tempted, were slain with the sword. They wandered about in sheepskins and goatskins, being destitute, afflicted, tormented–of whom the world was not worthy. They wandered in deserts and mountains, in dens and caves of the earth. And all these, having obtained a good testimony through faith, did not receive the promise, God

> having provided something better for us, that
> they should not be made perfect apart from us.

> Hebrews 11:35b–40

The writer to the Hebrews mentions suffering saints in chapter 11 as being an example for those of us who come along behind them. He points out that many believers suffered even before Jesus came, having not yet seen the promise of the Messiah. He reveals that those who suffered held tightly to their faith to the very end and, thereby, left us a witness written in blood. Then the writer goes on in Hebrews 12 to call on those of us living in the New Testament church age—who have so much more in the way of information, inspiration, and revelation from God—to lay aside every weight and the sin that easily overwhelms us so that we can run the Christian race with patience and perseverance. He reminds us that we can only do this while looking unto Jesus, the Author and Finisher of our faith. After all, Jesus endured the cross while looking forward to the joy that was set before Him. In other words, the Bible does not teach that the Christian life is free from suffering but that our faith must be bigger and better than our sorrows. In fact, those who suffer well for Jesus proclaim a faith that is not ankle deep, but a faith that will stand when one's life is flooded with tears and overwhelmed with a tsunami of sorrow. If we face our suffering with faith in God and dedication to Him, we will stand in the long line of saints who have, in the midst of many sorrows, kept the faith once delivered to the saints.

CAN YOU AND I LEAVE A TESTIMONY THROUGH SUFFERING?

In Hebrews 12:1, the Bible writer speaks of a *great cloud of witnesses*. Some have taken this passage to mean that you and I are running the race of life while those who have gone on to be with the Lord are watching us from above. That is not the meaning contained in this passage. There are two words in Koine Greek, the language used almost exclusively in the New Testament documents, for the word *witness*. One of the Greek words is *theati*, from which we get the English word *theater*. The other word for *witness* is the word *martur*, from which we get the English word *martyr*. In Hebrews 12:1, the writer used the word *martyr* and not the word *theater* when speaking of the *great cloud of witnesses*. In other words, the saints the writer is speaking of are not those who have gone to heaven and are now watching us here on earth; rather, they are the ones who have left us surrounded with a martyr's testimony written in their blood—they are those martyred for their faith in the Lord. They poured out all they had for the cause of the Lord, and their dedication is like a cloud surrounding us with a testimony of faithfulness. If you go to a college basketball arena or a major-league baseball stadium, you will see flags or jersey numbers hanging from the rafters or walls. They display the memory of those who played faithfully in the past to be a reminder to those who come behind. In the spiritual arena, God has placed around us the memory of those who suffered faithfully in His cause. The memory of these faithful servants is meant to spur us on as we now take their place in the work of God. The memory of their devotion calls out to remind us that we too must give our best in all circumstances in order to honor the Lord.

The great question for us today is whether we can so dedicate our lives now that we will leave a sacrificial testimony to the generation coming behind us. We cannot do that if we try to avoid every hardship in the service of the Lord. By any estimate, our lives today are easy compared to those who came before us, and we cannot allow ourselves to think that God's will is for us to suffer no trials while living for Him in these days.

Do You Also Want to Go Away?

In John 6, we read about one of the great miracles recorded in the New Testament. John describes Jesus feeding more than five thousand people with a little's boy lunch. The food the boy carried was barely enough for him to eat, but he gave it to the disciples, and Jesus used it to feed the great multitude. Jesus multiplied what was given, and that is what He always does with that which we are willing to entrust to Him. Jesus knew something about the crowd that He fed that day that others did not readily see. The crowd was following Him for what He gave them and not because they knew He was the Savior and Lord from heaven. At that point, Jesus said something to the crowd that was following Him, and what He said disturbed them greatly:

> Then Jesus said to them, "Most assuredly, I say to you, unless you eat the flesh of the Son of Man and drink His blood, you have no life in you. Whoever eats My flesh and drinks My

blood has eternal life, and I will raise him up at the last day. For My flesh is food indeed, and My blood is drink indeed. He who eats My flesh and drinks My blood abides in Me, and I in him. As the living Father sent Me, and I live because of the Father, so he who feeds on Me will live because of Me. This is the bread which came down from heaven–not as your fathers ate the manna, and are dead. He who eats this bread will live forever."

John 6:53–58

When the people heard this, they were troubled, and we are told in John 6:66 that they turned away and ceased following Jesus. They just could not understand how it was possible that they were to eat the flesh of Jesus and drink His blood. They enjoyed the buffet of fish and loaves that He supplied but could not trust Him when it came to difficult statements they could not understand.

In John 6:67, Jesus asked His disciples, "Do you also want to go away?" Peter answered that they had no one else to whom they could go; after all, Jesus alone had the words of life eternal.

The point here is that the Christian life is not about understanding everything. The people following Jesus for the wrong reasons turned back and left Him when they faced situations that they could not understand. Those who knew that He was the only one who could give them eternal life did not trouble themselves with things beyond their comprehension. If you will only serve Jesus when everything goes your way or when you can get an answer to every problem and question, you will never be a true follower of Christ.

Jesus could have explained what He meant when He told the crowd that they had to eat His flesh and drink His blood. We know what that means. We are familiar with the Lord's Supper and Communion. We know that Jesus was speaking figuratively. Note that Jesus did not explain the details or meaning of His statement to the crowd. He was testing their faith. We will experience things in our own lives that we cannot explain. Why does God allow us to go through so many difficulties? Why does he allow the faithful Christian to suffer divorce, children to grow up to live rebellious lives, financial hardships, bodily pains, and diseases? No one can answer those questions for you, and God will not likely tell you either. You will have to trust that He knows, and His way is the right way for your life. We cannot expect every question to be answered, and we are not to expect that our path will be covered with rose pedals. Jesus walked the Via Dolorosa, and He tells us to take up our cross and follow Him.

WE NEED THIRD-CLASS SENIOR ADULTS CHRISTIANS TODAY!

There is a story I read somewhere from the stagecoach days of the Old West. A man walked up to a ticket window to purchase passage on a stagecoach to Kansas City, Kansas. The price list revealed three levels and three prices to ride the stagecoach. There was a first-class ticket, a second-class ticket, and a third-class ticket listed. The prices ranged from very expensive for a first-class ticket to a quite reasonable price for a third-class ticket. The man asked the agent if the people with a third-class ticket got to ride inside the coach with the people holding a first-class ticket. The agent answered that everyone rode inside the coach. Then the man asked if those with a third-class ticket got to go all the way to Kansas City. The agent said that they did. So the man bought a third-class ticket and complimented himself on his financial frugality.

The stagecoach arrived, and all the passengers got inside for the journey to Kansas City. Indeed, they all rode in the same comfortable compartment of the coach. After a while, it began to rain, and the stagecoach came to a steep hill. The horses pulled for all they were worth, but they could not pull the loaded stagecoach up the hill through the thick mud. The driver got off the stagecoach, opened the door, and spoke to the riders. "All right," he said, "everyone with a first-class ticket stay where you are, those with a second-class ticket get out and walk, and those with a third-class ticket get out and *push!*"

Our churches are burdened at times with people who want to be first-class members. They want to ride while others walk or push. We need to be *third-class* Christians who are willing to help *push* the work of God along, even if it means enduring suffering for His namesake. And this includes remaining faithful to the cause of Christ and being upbeat in our attitude, even through our own personal sufferings.

Glory-Bound Debtors

In Romans 8, Paul shares something that helped him remain faithful throughout his many hardships, and he wrote to encourage us to have this same attitude in our lives. In Romans 8:12, we read, "Therefore, brethren, we are debtors—not to the flesh, to live according to the flesh." And then he wrote in Romans 8:18, "For I consider that the sufferings of this present time are not worthy to be compared with the glory which shall be revealed in us."

Paul saw himself as being in debt, not to please the flesh, but to please the Lord and walk in the Spirit of God. Christ paid for our sins at Calvary, and we owe everything to Him. If we think that the church or others owe us special deference, we will avoid hardship and seek to please our own flesh; but if we see ourselves as debtors to God and bound to a life in the Spirit, we will do what God asks of us regardless of the cost.

How can we maintain such an attitude? After all, no one really enjoys suffering and adversity. Paul reminds us that we are bound for glory. He clearly states that any suffering we are enduring here is not to be compared with the glory that awaits us. There was a time when Christians sang about and thought about heaven a lot. We have become so at ease in the world that heaven is not in the forefront of our thinking, preaching, and studying in this modern era. Some have commented that you hardly hear a preacher talk about hell in a sermon these days. That may be true, but you don't hear many sermons about heaven either. Sadly, many Christians are caught up today in the here and now. If we forget that we are pilgrims here on this earth and that we are true citizens of heaven, we will do all we can to avoid suffering. Don't forget whose you are, who you are, and where you are going. Be willing to get out of the coach and help push. At the top of the hill, we will be home with God!

No one can adequately explain suffering. In fact, we are not meant to understand why everything happens to us the way it does. It has always been a mystery as to why those who are unrighteous sometimes prosper and those who are righteous do not. Regardless of the circumstances, however, we are to be found faithful. As the songwriter said, "We'll understand it better by and by."[19] If you don't believe that, it is highly unlikely that you will suffer honorably for the Lord or that you will be faithful to Him in all of life's circumstances.

THE KINGDOM INCREASED THROUGH SUFFERING

In the book of Acts 5, we read that Peter and the disciples were arrested because they were teaching and preaching about Jesus.

> So they departed from the presence of the council, rejoicing that they were counted worthy to suffer shame for His name. And daily in the temple, and in every house, they did not cease teaching and preaching Jesus as the Christ.
>
> Acts 5:41–42

Did you notice in this text that the disciples rejoiced that they were counted *worthy* to suffer for *His name*? I have seen many Christians fall by the wayside because they got their feelings hurt at church. One who quits serving the Lord in a local fellowship of believers because his or her feelings were hurt should be ashamed. Everyone who serves the Lord will suffer at some point. It is unlikely, however, that anyone will beat you with whips because of your service for Christ, but the early disciples counted it a joy to suffer for Jesus and went right on doing His will and sharing His Word. All of us must brush the chips off our shoulders when it comes to serving Christ.

There was a positive aspect to suffering that the faithful disciples endured for Christ. Because they suffered with the right spirit, something wonderful happened. In Acts 6:1 (the verse that follows Acts 5:42), we read about the results of the suffering and service of those faithful disciples. Acts 6:1 reads, "Now in those days…the number of the disciples was multiplying." Wow! The faithful suffering of those disciples and their willingness to go on joyfully in His work led multitudes to faith in Christ. Their faithful suffering actually had a positive effect upon the kingdom of God. When we suffer hardships and insults with the right attitude and proper dedication, it can lead to great success in God's work.

If the focus of the Christian life is self-centered, suffering will not be tolerated. On the other hand, if the focus of the Christian life is to honor Jesus and obey Him in all circumstances, we will help bring people to faith in Christ. Suffering for Jesus must be seen as a badge of honor rather than a personal insult.

It is through hardships, trials, and suffering that people are drawn to Christ. It is interesting that the church, the universal church of all true believers, grows more rapidly in areas where Christians suffer than in areas of the world where Christians dominate and are at ease. We may not like to suffer (who really does?), but we must be willing to go through personal hardships to show that our faith is real. When we face our troubles with joy, God uses those troubles to touch others and bring them to faith in Jesus. It happened in the early church, and it happens around the world today. Sadly, many of us see the local church as a place where everyone should be accommodating to our needs rather than seeing it as a place where we are to take up our cross and follow Jesus.

When God's people are willing to suffer hardship in His service and continue to rejoice and serve faithfully, it creates an atmosphere that draws people to Jesus. Note that the disciples did not become angry when they suffered—they rejoiced! Faithfulness in the midst of hardship is of little value unless we maintain the right attitude. One lady was upset with her pastor about some decision the church had made. She was talking to a friend and said, "I don't care if the devil is in the pulpit, I'm not leaving my church." That is not the attitude of steadfast service that God has in mind for His people, and it is certainly not an attitude that will lead people to trust Jesus. We are to keep praising the Lord in all circumstances. We must also maintain a heart of love toward others. The disciples continued to preach and teach about Jesus without becoming bitter toward those who had beaten them.

When Stephen was being stone to death by his enemies, he begged God not to place upon them the charge for his death (Acts 7:59–60). That is why God was able to work through his life and the lives of the other disciples. The kind, gracious, and merciful attitude they maintained brought many people into the kingdom of God. If our churches expect to see people accepting Jesus Christ as Savior, the members will have to think less of themselves and more about honoring Christ in the good times and bad.

Suffer Application

Name at least two ways that people willingly suffer in life:

1. _____

2. _____

If we suffer as we should, we will grow _____ and not grow bitter.

In which Bible book and chapter do we discover amazing details about those who suffered gladly for the Lord?

Bible book:

_____

Chapter:

_____

In Hebrews, chapter 12, the scripture states that we are surrounded by a great cloud of witnesses. Which of the following is correct?

_____The sufferers have gone to heaven and are watching us as we live.

_____The sufferers left a testimony in blood that reminds us to be faithful.

If we pray faithfully, God will explain to us the reason for everything we are going through.

_____ True

_____ False

What does it mean to be a third-class Christian?

It means to get out and _____.

Paul reminded us that our suffering here cannot be compared to the _____ to be revealed in heaven.

Is it possible that God will call upon us to suffer in ways we cannot understand in order to complete His work in us, accomplish His will through us, and allow us to be a greater part of His plan for this world?

_____ Yes, that is likely.

_____ No, I don't think God would do that.

FOCUS

If you follow any sports, you are aware of how important it is to focus. Many times in sports events—whether it is golf, baseball, football, or others—the reporter will note that the game was lost because a player failed to keep his focus. The football receiver looks away before the ball reaches his hands, or the golfer's head comes up just before he hits the ball, or the baseball player looks away just before the grounder reaches his glove, and the game is lost.

My daughter, Sherry, does cross-stitching. She creates the most beautiful images, many of which are accompanied by Scripture verses. In order to do that as well as she does, it requires her complete focus on every stitch. My wife has done quilting, and the same thing is true in that process. They must place all of their attention on the process in order for their crafts to come out looking the way they are supposed look. The ability to focus is necessary if one is to be successful at any task.

The loss of focus leads to disaster. Some years ago a plane crashed, killing everyone on board, as it came into the Charlotte, North Carolina, airport. During the investigation, it was discovered that the pilot and copilot were gazing out the window and discussing a nearby theme park as they were on the landing path. I never heard for sure if that was the cause of the crash, but I think you would agree with me that all of us want the pilots to be totally focused on landing the plane when we are on a flight about ready to touch down on the runway.

Focus is especially true in the Christian life. Remember, the absence of focus is the most dangerous when it is lost at the last moment. For us as senior adults, we must remain focused on the Lord till we meet Him face-to-face. This requires discipline and dedication.

We read in 1 Kings 11:4 about King Solomon and the loss of his focus on the Lord in his last days. Mistakes in youth can often be corrected because there is time remaining in life to prove one's dedication; however, when focus is lost in the last years of life, that failure may be the only legacy many people will remember. Solomon was said to be a man of great wisdom, but even the wise can fail terribly if they do not keep their focus on the Lord and His will all the way to the end.

> For it was so, when Solomon was old, that his wives turned his heart after other gods; and his heart was not loyal to the Lord his God, as was the heart of his father David.
>
> 1 Kings 11:4

It is a sad thing to tarnish one's witness and testimony at any point in life, but it is especially dreadful to do so in one's senior years. Solomon had been so blessed by the Lord and had been given the gift of wisdom from the Lord; however, he failed to maintain a dedicated walk with God in His last years. Solomon knew the Lord and belonged to Him, as Scripture clearly indicates. We are told that Solomon was not *loyal to the Lord his God.* You will note that the *Lord* was Solomon's God, but Solomon was unfaithful to Him in his last days. Even those who know the Lord can make terrible mistakes late in life. As senior Christians, we need to guard against wrecking our witness. What can cause a mature Christian to fail and tarnish his or her testimony late in life?

RELAXATION CAN LEAD TO RUIN

Solomon lost his focus because he relaxed his commitment. Perhaps Solomon had become so cozy in life that he abandoned the sense of being God's representative. It appears that he was so apathetic and indifferent about His relationship to God that he allowed himself to be led astray.

Two boys were sitting at the back of a classroom in an English class. The teacher said, "There is one simple reason to explain why the students in this class are not doing well in English." She then turned and wrote one word, in very large letters, on the white board: APATHY.

One boy turned to the other and slowly tried to read the word. "A...pa...thy," and he followed that by asking,

"What in the world does that mean?" The other boy lazily said, "Who knows and who cares."

Maybe Solomon had reached the point that he didn't know how dangerous his behavior was, or he just didn't care. One doesn't have to be in full rebellion to get into trouble with the Lord. Apathy and indifference are enough to lead us to ruin. It is possible that Solomon simply cared more about Solomon than he did about the Lord and the Lord's cause. If that was the case, one could say that Solomon was a chip off the old block.

Solomon's father was King David. Almost everyone knows the story of David and Bathsheba. David had an affair with Bathsheba after seeing her from his rooftop one evening as she bathed. David sent for her, and a sordid affair began between them. Bathsheba was married to one of David's faithful soldiers at the time of the affair. When Bathsheba became pregnant with David's child, David tried to cover up the matter by having Bathsheba's husband, Uriah, come home from battle in the hope that he would be with Bathsheba, and this would lead Uriah to think that the child Bathsheba was carrying was his own. Uriah, however, would not go home to spend the night with his wife while his fellow soldiers were still on the front lines of battle. So David sent Uriah back to the battlefield and gave instructions for the commander to leave Uriah in the forefront of the fighting so that he would be killed in battle. Everything went as David planned. Well, almost everything went as he had planned. Eventually, Nathan the prophet came to David and confronted him about the sin. You can be sure that your sins will find you out (Numbers 32:23).

It is very difficult for us to imagine David, a man after God's own heart, doing such horrible things, but this event reminds us that no one is immune to temptations and sins of the very worst kind. A king's palace provides no special protection from the danger of sin. If we lose our focus, relax our souls, and unlock our hearts, we will find sin crouching at the door, and a flood of iniquity will pour in without regard to the person or the place involved (Genesis 4:7). Sin is like water; it searches for the path of least resistance and rushes in without hesitation at any and every opportunity. A person's position, wealth, and intelligence does not ensure protection if places are left unsealed around the walls, roof, and windows of the heart and mind; likewise, King David's palace life was not sealed up properly, and a flood of sin poured into David's life and did immeasurable damage in the process!

Where was the unsealed area in David's life that led to the sins of adultery, lying, and manslaughter? If we read the story carefully, we can see how the downward process began in David's life.

> It happened in the spring of the year, at the time when kings go out to battle, that David sent Joab and his servants with him, and all Israel; and they destroyed the people of Ammon and besieged Rabbah. But David remained at Jerusalem. Then it happened one evening that David arose from his bed and walked on the roof of the king's house. And from the roof

> he saw a woman bathing, and the woman was very beautiful to behold. So David sent and inquired about the woman. And someone said, "Is this not Bathsheba, the daughter of Eliam, the wife of Uriah the Hittite?" Then David sent messengers, and took her; and she came to him, and he lay with her, for she was cleansed from her impurity; and she returned to her house. And the woman conceived; so she sent and told David, and said, "I am with child."
>
> 2 Samuel 11:1–5

There is a telltale sign in this Bible passage from 2 Samuel as to what led David to commit these awful and appalling sins. Note in verse 1 that the time came for kings to go into battle, but David sent Joab and the troops out to fight while he remained at his palace. The text states, "But David remained in Jerusalem." Had David become so comfortable in his palace that he no longer felt a need to join his men on the battlefield? It certainly seems that way. The comfort of his position as king, his power to delegate, and the coziness of his palace most likely led David to be on his balcony the night when Bathsheba bathed below his window. *His relaxation led to his rebellion! The loss of divine focus led to a failure in faithfulness.*

David was still relatively young when he committed this sin with Bathsheba, and that meant he had time to recommit his life to the Lord and restore his reputation as a servant of the Lord. You can read David's confession and renewal in Psalm 32 and Psalm 51. The pleasure of sin can last for a moment and require costs that last for years. Note David's confession:

> Purge me with hyssop, and I shall be clean;
> Wash me, and I shall be whiter than snow.
> Make me hear joy and gladness,
> That the bones You have broken may rejoice.
> Hide Your face from my sins,
> And blot out all my iniquities.
>
> Psalm 51:7–9

David experienced pain so great, as a result of his sin, that it made him feel as if some of his bones were broken. Anyone who knows the full story of David's life is aware that his sin brought sorrow to him and to his family for many years.

When I was a boy, my friends and I made wooden motorless carts and rode them recklessly down steep hills between trees in the woods. One day I rode down a steep hill on my cart, turning between trees, when suddenly my cart flipped up on one side. I put out my hand to keep from pounding my head into one of the trees, and the thumb on my right hand hit the trunk of the tree. I was immediately thrust into intense pain. I could see the broken bone through the skin, and the throbbing pain only got worse as I hurried out of the woods to find help. I got to the doctor's office, and he confirmed what I already knew—the large bone at the back of my thumb was definitely broken. The orthopedic doctor did surgery on the bone and created a contraption to keep it in traction for six weeks. I endured the agony of healing that seemed to go on forever! But that is not the whole story. Even now, my thumb will ache terribly on certain days. It is a reminder for all my days of a foolish act when I was a child. Sure, the thumb was set by an excellent doctor and every effort was made to fix the problem, but even the best doctor in the world could not remove the consequences of my action. Likewise, when we sin and we confess our wrongdoing to the Lord, He forgives us (1 John 1:9). However, the consequences of our sin can remain with us the rest of our lives. It is not that God is punishing us; rather, it is a fact that our human actions have long-term consequences. David learned this lesson the hard way.

God is a God of grace, and thus David found forgiveness from God. David went on to live a dedicated life for the Lord in his remaining years. It is good to remember that God is the God of the second chance— and third chance, and fourth chance, and fifth chance, etc. But if one soils his or her testimony for the Lord late in life, it can be too late to renew a solid testimony. Sin late in life is no worse than sin early in life; sin is sin! But sin late in life is much worse in one sense—it has the potential of leaving behind a sullied testimony and pollutes an otherwise positive witness for the Lord.

The point is that David may well have committed his awful sin of adultery and manslaughter because he relaxed his commitment and values, and it seems that Solomon sinned for the same reason. But for Solomon, there was no time remaining for him to create a renewed testimony of His love for God. He was old when he turned to other gods, and that left him little time to show those around him that his faith in God was real!

Senior adult Christians are always in danger of becoming comfortable and at ease. We need to be reminded that life is not all about us. We can become self-centered and focus only on our needs and desires. This is true in our church life as well. Many senior adults want the church to keep things the way they have always been, and they desire that people in the church cater to their desires and wishes. This kind of thinking leads to many problems in our lives at home, in the community, and in the church fellowship. We must focus on God's will, His work, and His glory if we would be effective servants of the Lord all the way to the end!

Solomon left a stain on his testimony. Many older Christians are guilty of doing things in the last years of their lives that is similar to leaving an ugly stain on an otherwise beautiful garment; the stain takes the attention away from the beauty that once graced the garment. The most expensive well-made suit or dress on earth is of little value if it has a stain that cannot be removed. We must work at maintaining the beauty of holiness in our lives, especially when we are older. Note what Jesus said about His bride, the church:

> That He might present her to Himself a glorious church, not having spot or wrinkle or any such thing, but that she should be holy and without blemish. So husbands ought to love their own wives as their own bodies; he who loves his wife loves himself.
>
> Ephesians 5:27–28

Jesus cleansed us when we trusted Him as Savior and Lord. He washed us and made us pure. His intention is to present us in heaven as a "glorious church, not having sport of wrinkle." We must take seriously the responsibility to remain faithful to Him all the days of our lives.

You Will Change That Over My Dead Body!

A church was in the process of making a decision regarding one of the church programs. One senior adult stood and opposed it and did so with a very ugly attitude. The senior Christian said as she finished her remarks, "You may change this when I am dead and gone, but you will only change it now over my dead body!" There was no concern in this lady's heart as to whether the change would help young Christians grow or whether the change would bring lost souls to Christ; her only concern was her opinion about the issue and her comfort level in her church. Long after this lady had passed away, the memory of her words reverberated though that church. They were repeated by people who sadly remembered her only through those words. No doubt she had served the Lord in positive ways through the years, but what people remembered was her statement in that church business meeting near the end of her earthly life. What a shame! She had stained her testimony at the end.

I have seen this happen during my long ministry in the local church. I was pastoring a church early in my ministerial days when a sad incident occurred. An elderly woman who had served the Lord for many years in the local church was still in charge of a particular church ministry. Her young assistant wanted to change one of the rooms used in this work. The change the young assistant was asking for was minor and would certainly have been an improvement, but the elderly leader opposed it. The young assistant came to me and shared her frustration. I agreed to meet with them to discuss the matter. In that meeting, the elderly lady said, "I don't care what you do about this after I am gone, but it will not be done while I'm in charge." The elderly leader did not argue that the change wasn't needed or that it would not improve the program; she just didn't want anyone to touch what had become sacred to her. I told the young assistant to leave everything the way it was because the change she wanted was not worth the fight that would ensue. Before long, the elderly lady passed away, and the next day, plans were put into action to make the change. Once completed, the change improved the program and made the entire operation more flexible for everyone involved. What a sad story! Every time the memory of that senior adult lady crosses my mind, I can't help but remember her stubborn resistance to a simple change. I don't want to remember her that way, but it is simply a testimony she left behind that is difficult to erase.

SELFISHNESS CAN LEAD TO RUIN

In Isaiah 39, we read about King Hezekiah, who was the king of Judah during the days of Isaiah. King Hezekiah entertained a delegation from Babylon and showed them all the treasures of gold and silver in the House of Judah. Isaiah told Hezekiah that the day was coming when all the treasures of Judah would be taken away by the Babylonians and that this would happen to his sons. In other words, the loss of the treasures of Judah would not occur until Hezekiah was dead. Note verse 8 in Isaiah 39: "So Hezekiah said to Isaiah, 'The word of the Lord which you have spoken is good!' For he said, 'At least there will be peace and truth in my days.'" In other words, Hezekiah didn't care what ills and troubles befell Judah after his death or how much misery his children would have to endure; he only cared about life being comfortable for him until he was gone. Hezekiah was plagued with the disease of comfort. We are in danger of thinking only about ourselves and our desires, and this danger is increased as we age. We must keep our focus on the God of the Kingdom and the Kingdom of God if we are to live for His glory and not our own.

What are some of the elements that lead to a loss of focus on God and His will?

ARROGANCE

Arrogance may well have been one factor that led Solomon to turn to other gods in his latter days. Pride goes before a fall (Proverbs 16:18). In other words, when pride enters the Christian heart, that Christian is on the precipice of disaster. Arrogance and pride are twins, and they are ugly twins indeed.

Pride was the first sin committed in the Garden of Eden. The serpent told Eve that she would be a god if she simply ate the fruit that God had denied her. Satan was appealing to Eve's pride in order to motivate her to sin against God.

While at Gardner Webb University, I witnessed to a young man, we will call him John, who seemed very open to the Gospel. One day John said he was ready to accept Jesus as his Savior. Just as we were about to pray together, a couple of John's friends walked up. I saw John's countenance change, and he looked at me and said, "I'll talk to you about this later." John walked away with his friends, and I never got the chance to talk to him again. John was embarrassed, and he allowed personal pride to keep him from accepting Jesus as his Savior. He allowed his friends to take his focus away from Christ and perhaps lost forever his opportunity to become a Christian.

Just as pride can delude those without Christ, pride can mislead those who know the Lord. David and Solomon sinned, not only because they took a laissez-faire attitude in regard to God's will, but also because of the pride involved in their positions and power as kings. In fact, the issues are not mutually exclusive; apathy and arrogance are often wed to one another, and they led David and Solomon to make decisions without consulting the Lord. That is how pride works; it leads a person to form an opinion without considering God's Word or God's will in the matter. In essence, pride puts self on the throne and attempts to put God in the shadows, and that is a recipe for disaster!

A believer who has served the Lord for a long time can begin to feel that he or she deserves to be treated with a deference that is not due to others. Senior Christians can feel that younger believers should always defer to their opinions and decisions. Yet when Jesus was asked by his disciples who was to be considered greatest in the Kingdom, He surprised them with His answer.

> At that time the disciples came to Jesus, saying, "Who then is greatest in the kingdom of heaven?" Then Jesus called a little child to Him, set him in the midst of them, and said, "Assuredly, I say to you, unless you are converted and become as little children, you will by no means enter the kingdom of heaven. Therefore whoever humbles himself as this little child is the greatest in the kingdom of heaven. Whoever receives one little child like this in My name receives Me."
>
> Matthew 18:1–5

KINGDOM PEOPLE ARE HUMBLE

Jesus pointed out that Kingdom people are humble and childlike. It is not unusual for disciples of Jesus to struggle for position and power within the church or within Christian circles. Sadly, once a Christian obtains a place of status, he or she will often use it as a means of domination over others. This is to be expected in secular society, but Christians should be different. We are to act in a loving and caring manner in keeping with the nature of Jesus.

> But Jesus called them to *Himself* and said, "You know that the rulers of the Gentiles lord it over them, and those who are great exercise authority over them. Yet it shall not be so among you; but whoever desires to become great among you, let him be your servant. And whoever desires to be

first among you, let him be your slave—just as the Son of Man did not come to be served, but to serve, and to give His life a ransom for many."

Matthew 20:25–28

I was speaking with a minister recently about this subject, and I asked him how many senior adult Christians he had known who reflected the nature of Jesus all the way to the end of their lives. I clarified my question by adding that I was speaking of senior Christians who kept a bright spirit, stayed away from gossip and infighting, and who bore a positive witness for Jesus all the way through to leaving this world to meet the Savior. The minister, who had pastored for many years, stopped and thought for moment. Then he began to name people. After about six or seven names, he said, "I think that about covers it." Wow! A lifetime of ministry and only a handful of older Christians could be recalled who reflected the love and nature of Jesus to the very end. If that minister had more time, I am sure he would have thought of a lot more names to share, but his response confirmed what I already knew—too few of us as Christians have reached our senior years properly reflecting the humble nature of our Lord.

What about you? Is your spiritual attitude toward other Christians and church leaders one of love and support? Do you find yourself complaining and arguing about issues that are not doctrinal or issues that do not have a direct biblical mandate? Do you get caught up in negative topics that others bring to your attention, or do you try your best to steer people toward a spirit of praise and joy in the Lord? These are important questions. To be sure, none of us are pleased with everything that happens in our homes or our churches. Differences of opinion are normal between family and friends. We cannot be close to people without some disagreement arising between us from time to time. In fact, most of us are not pleased with what we see in the mirror every morning! Most of us who are married don't agree with our spouse on everything either. A few married couples hardly agree on anything. The issue of disagreeing is not nearly as important as the attitude that we reflect in the disagreement. If we are to honor Jesus, we must show a Christ-like attitude.

As we grow older in the Lord, let's grow brighter, happier, more joyful, and more complimentary of His work and of each other. As senior Christians, we will be departing for home very soon, so let's get ready to meet our Savior and hear Him say, "Well done, thou good and faithful servant." Let's keep our focus on that which matters most! Some of us would do well to join in the following prayer found in *The Preacher's Quote Book*:

> Thou knowest I am growing older. Keep me from the idea that I must express myself on every subject. Release me from the craving to meddle in everyone's affair. Keep my tongue from the recital of endless details of the past which do not interest others. Seal my lips when I am inclined to talk about my aches and pains. They are increasing with the years, and my love to speak of them grows sweeter as time goes by. Teach me the glorious lesson that occasionally

I may be wrong. Make me thoughtful, but not interfering; helpful, but not bossy. With the wisdom and experience I've gained, it does seem a pity not to use it all, but Thou knowest, Lord, that I want a few friends left at the end. So help me to pray more, talk less. And beyond all this, let me continue to flourish spiritually and bring forth fruit to Thy glory even in old age. Amen![20]

DIE CLIMBING

If we focus on the Lord as we should, we can end our lives at the peak of Christian excellence. There is a story told about a Swiss mountain guide who loved to climb in the Alps. Though I have never seen the marker, I have read numerous accounts of the epitaph left on the mountainside in memory of the guide. It seems that he went out to climb among the Alps one day and did not return. Friends searched for him and found him dead along one of the mountain trails. They placed a marker at the spot to commemorate the mountain guide's life. The marker contained his name and the following words: He Died Climbing.[21]

That is what each of us ought to strive to do in our Christian lives. Keep climbing in your life and service for Jesus. It would be better to die on the way up a mountain of service for the Lord than to crumble in a heap of regret in some valley of failure. Keep climbing upward with a humble heart and dedicated spirit. We can make the last years of our lives the best years of our service to Jesus.

Henry W. Longfellow wrote,

Shall we sit idly down and say,
The night hath come; it is no longer day?
The night hath not yet come; we are not quite
Cut off from labor by the failing light;
Something remains for us to do or dare;
Even the oldest tree some fruit may bear.

Attentiveness Can Avoid Ruin

The secret to a happy Christian life, whether we are in our teens or in our eighties, is to remain close to Jesus—to keep our focus on Him and to be attentive to Him. Sadly, it is possible to become so familiar with the supernatural that it breeds an atmosphere of insipidness and boredom. We can lose the excitement of being redeemed and the blessing of being near the Redeemer. When the mysterious becomes mundane and the divine becomes drudgery, the Lord finds a way to shake us up and wake us up. The Lord promised never to leave us and never to forsake us, but that can be a warning as much as it is a blessing. Because He is always with us, He is very aware of our commitment level. He loves us, but that does not mean that He is always happy about the way we serve Him. When we become indifferent, He can become indignant! If we become apathetic, He can become annoyed! As our Father, He can decide that we need to visit the woodshed of discipline!

Wait Till Your Father Comes Home!

Did you ever do something wrong when you were a child and knew you were going to have to face your mom or dad about it? I can remember my mother saying to me, on more than one occasion, "Just wait till your dad gets home!"

Later, I would hear Dad pull into the driveway and close the door of the car. At that point, my nerves would be on edge. Then I would then hear the door close as he came into the house, and I could hear my dad and mom discussing something, and I knew what the discussion was about! By that time, I was in a full panic mode. And then I would hear my dad's footsteps coming toward my room. At that moment, even as a child, I would pray a premillennial prayer. "Even so, come, Lord Jesus!" I loved my father, but being near him at that moment was not my idea of a good, close relationship.

DIVINE DISCIPLINE

In Hebrews 12, we read about the discipline that God applies to His children when they are disobedient.

> "And scourges every son whom He receives." If you endure chastening, God deals with you as with sons; for what son is there whom a father does not chasten? But if you are without chastening, of which all have become partakers, then you are illegitimate and not sons. Furthermore, we have had human fathers who corrected us, and we paid them respect. Shall we not much more readily be in subjection to the Father of spirits and live? For they indeed for a few days chastened us as seemed best to them, but He for our profit, that we may be partakers of His holiness. Now no chastening seems to be joyful for the present, but painful; nevertheless, afterward it yields the peaceable

> fruit of righteousness to those who have been
> trained by it. Therefore strengthen the hands
> which hang down, and the feeble knees, and
> make straight paths for your feet.
>
> Hebrews 12:6–13

Clearly we are told in this passage that God chastises those who truly belong to Him. If you are acting, thinking, or speaking outside God's will and you sense no conviction or experience no chastisement from the Lord, you need to look closely as to whether you are truly a Christian. The writer to the Hebrews tells us that God chastens *every true child of God.* Note in verse 13 that we are told to *make straight paths for your feet.* We cannot walk the straight path if we are not following in His footsteps, nor can we do so if we are resisting His correction. As a child of my biological father, it was necessary for me to accept his correction. Likewise, as a child of God, I must submit to His discipline and correction. Some of us have resisted God's correction so often and for so long that we are out of fellowship with God and don't even know it. When my dad disciplined me, he would often say, "Son, look at me." He wanted my undivided attention. That is what God wants from us. We must keep our focus on Him!

HOW CAN I MAINTAIN MY FOCUS?

To remain close to Jesus, we have to follow in His footsteps. But how can I know what He wants me to do? How can I know His will? This is a question every minister of the Gospel is asked many times: *how can I know the will of God for my life?*

STAYING OR STRAYING?

We must stay close to Jesus if we expect to stay in His will. As I mentioned earlier in this book, when Jesus called His disciples, He said, "Come, follow me." That is what you and I are to do in every situation. If we do not stay close to Him, we will stray ever farther from His path for our lives. Just because we have been Christians for a long time does not mean that we are immune to drifting away from God's course for our lives.

- We can stray through wrong moral behavior.
- We can stray through improper finances and a lack of stewardship.
- We can stray through selfish and unchristian attitudes.
- We can stray through omitted or wishy-washy worship.
- We can stray through our failure to maintain a Christian witness.
- We can stray through a lackluster love for Him.
- We can stray through nonexistent communication with Him—a lack of prayer.
- We can stray through the presence of pride.

And there are many other areas where we can get off the right path. But there are some things we can do to stay on the right path. I want to spotlight three elements of knowing and doing God's will, three things that can help us remain close to Jesus all the way through to the end.

LOVE HIM

First, we must love Him. Love is more than an emotion; love involves commitment to the one loved. My wife does not want me to be committed to marriage; she wants me to be committed to *her!* In Revelation 2:4–5, we read these words from Jesus to the church at Ephesus:

> Nevertheless I have this against you, that you have left your first love. Remember therefore from where you have fallen; repent and do the first works, or else I will come to you quickly and remove your lampstand from its place— unless you repent.
>
> Revelation 2:4–5

Jesus walks among His people as the Great Physician; as a spiritual cardiologist, He gives each of us a daily heart exam. He is examining us to see if we have *left* the *first love*, the kind of love that ought to be present in our hearts and the type of love that ought to be displayed in our actions. He is the only one who knows the condition of our spiritual hearts. We can dress up on Sunday, sing the hymns, and pray the prayers in a worship service without really being in love with Jesus. Others around us may not know, but God knows! In fact, you don't likely even know your own heart. You may think that you do, but your heart can deceive you; however, our hearts cannot deceive Him! That is why the Psalmist prayed,

Search me, O God, and know my heart;
Try me, and know my anxieties;
And see if there is any wicked way in me,
And lead me in the way everlasting.

Psalm 139:23–24

Also, we read this in Jeremiah:

The heart is deceitful above all things,
And desperately wicked;
Who can know it?
I, the Lord , search the heart,
I test the mind,
Even to give every man according to his ways,
According to the fruit of his doings.

Jeremiah 7:9–10

Only the Lord knows the human heart. He states clearly that He, as Lord, is the only one who can *search the heart*. We need to open our hearts to Him and ask Him to search our hearts to see if there is any seed or sprout of wickedness growing there. If we are open to correction, He will surely reveal any coldness that appears in our hearts.

Following Jesus closely begins with the heart! How can I recommit my heart to the Lord? How can I bring back the fire of love if in fact it is missing in my heart?

REMEMBER

To discover if you love Jesus the way you should, just go back in your mind and remember the times when you were really close to Him. Most of us can recall a time when a fire burned in our hearts for the Lord.

We loved Him passionately and were ready to follow Him anywhere and to obey Him in doing everything He asked. Falling in love with the Lord all over again requires remembering or calling to mind, the times when our hearts were warm with affection for Him.

We just read in the book of Revelation how Jesus spoke to the church at Ephesus. He told them that they had left their first love. You will recall that Paul also wrote a letter to that church. At one point in Paul's letter, he spoke about love between a husband and wife, but he applied it to the love between Jesus and the church (all Christians).

> Husbands, love your wives, just as Christ also loved the church and gave Himself for her, that He might sanctify and cleanse her with the washing of water by the word, that He might present her to Himself a glorious church, not having spot or wrinkle or any such thing, but that she should be holy and without blemish. So husbands ought to love their own wives as their own bodies; he who loves his wife loves himself. For no one ever hated his own flesh, but nourishes and cherishes it, just as the Lord does the church. For we are members of His body, of His flesh and of His bones. "For this reason a man shall leave his father and mother and be joined to his wife, and the two shall become one flesh." This is a great mystery, but I speak concerning Christ and the church.
>
> Ephesians 5:25–33

Though Paul was writing to the Ephesians about the relationship between a husband and wife, he revealed something critical about Jesus and the church. In this passage, we read that Christ loved us so much that He gave Himself for us. In essence, Paul said the love between Jesus and His bride, the church, is crucial! We know Jesus loves us; after all, He gave Himself for us at Calvary. A greater question concerns how much we love Him. We will not follow Him appropriately if we do not love Him fully!

When a married couple develops a problem in their relationship, one of the best things a counselor can do is help them remember what it was like when they first fell in love. If the couple begins to rehearse memories of when and where they met, their first date, and some other early memories, it can often rekindle the old fire that once burned with a blue flame in their hearts. Likewise, when you and I become *cold* in our love relationship with the Lord, we are called upon in Revelation 2:5 to *remember*. As we remember how lost we were when the Lord found us and the awful price He paid to redeem us, it helps stir a renewed love for Jesus in our hearts.

In the Old Testament, God often required people to set up stone monuments as a source of reminding them of His deliverance and blessings from the past. It is easy for us to forget God's goodness toward us, and that forgetfulness leads us to become self-centered and self-reliant. If we decide we can make it without His leadership and wisdom, He will allow us to fall on our faces. But it is His desire for us to focus on Him, to remember Him, and to remain close to Him. We must not grow so familiar in our relationship to the Lord that we take for granted His blessings. By remembering how wonderful God has been to us, we go back to monuments in our hearts; we go back to special times and places when our love for Jesus was burning within us. If we fail to remember, the love in our hearts for the Lord will flicker, and hearts will grow cold.

> So it shall be, when the Lord your God brings you into the land of which He swore to your fathers, to Abraham, Isaac, and Jacob, to give you large and beautiful cities which you did not build, houses full of all good things, which you did not fill, hewn-out wells which you did not dig, vineyards and olive trees which you did not plant—when you have eaten and are full—*then* beware, lest you forget the Lord who brought you out of the land of Egypt, from the house of bondage.
>
> Deuteronomy 6:10–12

God's warning was clear to those who had escaped bondage in Egypt. He had blessed them greatly. He used His power to deliver them, but the Lord knew the danger that lay ahead. He told them that once they began to enjoy greater blessings in the Promised Land, there was the likelihood that they would forget Him. We need to remember the words "Beware, lest you forget the Lord."

Those who have been blessed the most by the Lord are at risk of developing spiritual dementia—

forgetfulness. Take a moment and remember God's blessings to you. Don't forget all He has done and is doing in your life. Think right now about times in the past when you were very close to the Lord. Can you remember those times? Maybe it was a time of old-fashioned revival. Perhaps it was when your children were born or when you experienced some unique forgiveness from or restoration to the Lord. It was likely a time so special that tears fell as you prayed. You seemed to float through the day because His presence was so real to you. Would you like for that closeness to be renewed? Bow and confess that you are not as close to Him as you once were. Thank Him for loving you through everything you have experienced. Ask Him to fill you with His love and joy. Even if you don't sense Him doing that immediately, if you are sincere, a day will come soon when you will experience in your heart an invigorating joy from God's throne! Your love will be intensified and renewed.

REPENT
Remembering past experiences is not enough for a full renewal of love. It is important to be honest with Jesus. We must repent of the coldness of our hearts toward Him. Repenting means to turn around and move in the right direction.

I have a GPS system in my car that helps me find the correct route when driving. Occasionally, I will miss a turn that the GPS has advised that I take. When I miss a turn, the GPS guidance system will speak in a warm female voice, saying, "Please make a U-turn as soon as it is safe." God does that to us as well. When we move in the wrong direction, He speaks to us and tells us to turn around—to repent.

Repenting involves changing one's behavior and attitude. When God reveals to you that the way you are acting, talking, or thinking is inappropriate, it is not enough to just admit it to Him; you need to change it! When we are willing to turn from the things in our lives that disappoint our Lord, we find ourselves in a closer walk with Him.

Sins do not separate Christians from their relationship to Christ, but our sins can negatively affect our *fellowship* with Christ. When I failed my human father, it did not remove me from being his son. My father's blood ran through my veins. However, when I failed him, it did cause a fellowship problem with my father. Sin against our heavenly Father works much the same way. When I sin against the Lord, I do not lose my position as His child; however, my sin does affect my fellowship with Him.

Sin causes us to walk at a distance from the Lord, and we must repent in order to renew a close walk with Christ. Repenting doesn't necessarily mean that anyone but God has to know about it. We can confess our sin to the Lord privately. However, there are times when our sin is public and involves others. When we sin against others, we should not only confess it to God, but we must go to the person or persons we have offended and make it right. Doing that is called restitution, and it is part of honest repentance. You and I can deal with our sins without publicly airing them, but when our sin has become a public matter, we need to stand and deal with them openly.

A Christian college student became pregnant. She didn't want to compound her sin by having an abortion, so the decision was made for her to have the child. She had been a leader among the youth in the church before going to college, and her mother and father were leaders at the time of this incident. Because she was pregnant, her sinful behavior would soon be known to everyone. The young lady took the bold step of standing before the large congregation to confess her sin to God and to ask for His forgiveness and the forgiveness of the church family. The love that poured forth from the members of the church for her and her family blessed me beyond measure. That young lady went on to have a beautiful baby, married one of the finest young men in the church, and today they have a lovely family. In addition, her husband adopted her child and made it his own. Today they serve God faithfully and provide an example of confession, repentance, and love that all of us can copy. Every time I think of them, my heart is filled with joy.

When we love God, are honest with Him, and honest with others, He can take what appears to be failure and turn it into victory. On the other hand, if we are too proud to confess our sins and repent, we damage our fellowship with God, and our usefulness in His cause is greatly diminished.

RETURN

Jesus told the Christians in the church at Ephesus to "do the first works" (Revelation 2:5). In other words,

He tells them to go back to the way it was when they first knew Him as Lord and Savior. What are the first works? Faith and love! We were saved when we placed our faith in Him and returned to Him the love He first had for us.

I remember my call to the ministry better than I remember my salvation experience. I was very young when I was saved, and it was real to me, but I can remember even more clearly my call to the ministry because I was a little older at that time. When I was twelve years old, our church had a week of revival services, and it was a wonderful meeting, one that my father and mother often mentioned as the greatest revival week they ever experienced. One night during that revival, I knew that Christ was calling me to preach His Word. I was frightened by the prospect, but I was also set on fire within. I told my parents and my preacher about my decision. The revival week was going so well, and so many decisions were being made that my commitment resulted in a basic pat on the head with comments like "That's fine. We are happy for you."

The revival services ran from Sunday morning through Friday evening. I woke up on Saturday morning hating that the revival services were over. You know it had to be a grand revival meeting if a twelve-year-old boy didn't want it to end. Most of the time, it is difficult to get twelve-year-old boys to go to church, but I was grieving because we were not going to have a Saturday night service.

On the Saturday morning following the revival, I woke up before anyone at my house. I ate some cereal, dressed, and walked about a mile to my preacher's house. I pounded on his door—it was about 7:00 a.m.—and waited for someone to answer. I had no idea how exhausted the pastor must have been after a weeklong revival. I finally heard someone stirring inside and then footsteps heading for the door. The pastor opened the door in his pajamas with his hair disheveled and looking like a ghost.

"Michael," he gasped, "is something wrong?"

"No," I answered, "I just thought I would come by and talk to you."

"Uh, okay," he replied while rubbing his sleepy-looking eyes. "Come on in."

His wife stumbled into the kitchen asking if everything was okay. Once I told her that I just wanted to talk to the pastor and there was no real emergency, she didn't look all that excited to have me at her house at 7:00 a.m. on Saturday. At any rate, I sat at the kitchen table and ate a second breakfast as I told the pastor that I had hardly slept the night before. He didn't say it, but he was probably thinking, *Well, I didn't sleep much either. Some crazy kid was knocking on my door at 7:00 a.m.*! But if he felt way, he didn't show it. He seemed really excited and spent much of the morning talking with me.

I was so in love with Jesus following that revival. My love for Christ was like a flame in my heart. Whenever I want to *remember*, I can go back to moments like the ones I experienced during and after that revival. As I look back on wonderful spiritual high points in my life, I pray, *Jesus, do I love you like that today? If not, am I willing to repent and return to you with full devotion? Am I willing to refocus my heart on you?* I cannot follow Him closely if I do not love Him deeply! Loving Him deeply involves remembering, repenting, and returning.

We are reminded of the danger of allowing our love for Jesus to grow cold and indifferent. In Revelation 2:5, Jesus tells the Christians at Ephesus to return to their first love or He will come and remove their *candlestick*. There is a lot of debate concerning the nature of the candlestick mentioned in that verse; however, there is one thing we know for sure: in those days, candlesticks were critical for seeing after the sun went down. There were no electric lights, and oil lanterns were the only means of light. Without a light from burning oil, one was simply walking in the dark.

If you and I leave our first love, our true love for Jesus, we will walk in the dark. That means that we will not have a sense of the will of God for our lives. So let's go back to the initial question: *how can we know God's will?* The most important step in the process of discovering God's will is to be sure you have a true active love for Jesus.

My wife and I will celebrate our fiftieth wedding anniversary this year. I don't have to ask her what she likes and doesn't like. She loves me, and I love her. I know what she enjoys, what she likes to eat, even the perfume she likes to wear. If you really love Jesus, you can sense what He wants you to do, and you understand that He knows your need even before you ask Him. Closeness to Jesus opens to you a clearer understanding of His will. We simply must desire a close walk with Jesus if you want to find God's purpose for us.

What you love, you will focus on intensely. What you focus on intensely, you will understand more fully. So when you love Jesus deeply, you focus on Him. When you focus on Him more fully, you begin to have a better understanding of what He is doing and how you can walk in the center of His will. Loving Him does not involve getting Him to do what we want Him to do; loving Him involves shaping our lives to do that which He wants us to do. That is what it means to know and do God's will.

Have you ever loved Jesus more at anytime in your life than you love Him right now? Be honest! Perhaps it is time to renew your love toward Him. As you do, you will find a light on your path that may have been missing for a while.

BE FILLED WITH THE SPIRIT

There are some who say that being in love with Jesus and being filled with the Spirit are one and the same. To a certain extent, that is true, but only because one who is filled with the Spirit cannot help but be in love with Jesus. Being filled with the Spirit is not really an option for a Christian; it is commanded in Scripture.

> Therefore do not be unwise, but understand what the will of the Lord is and do not be drunk with wine, in which is dissipation; but be filled with the Spirit, speaking to one another in psalms and hymns and spiritual songs, singing and making melody in your heart to the Lord,

> giving thanks always for all things to God the Father in the name of our Lord Jesus Christ, submitting to one another in the fear of God.
>
> Ephesians 5:17–21

The Bible plainly tells us that it is the will of God for us to be filled with the Spirit of God. It is absolutely *unwise* to fail in this matter. Many Christians do not understand this issue, and because of that, they simply ignore it. Every Christian needs to deal with this matter on a personal basis.

CONTROL

Control. The first issue related to being filled with the Spirit of God is the matter of control. We are told in this passage not to be intoxicated with alcohol, but to be filled with the Spirit. Paul used this contrast between a person being intoxicated and a person being filled with the Spirit to reveal what being filled with the Spirit actually means. If a person is filled with alcohol, he or she is *controlled* by the substance. A person intoxicated walks differently, talks differently, and acts differently than he or she would when sober. The alcohol takes control. Likewise, when a person is filled with the Spirit of God, he or she is controlled by the Lord. Thought, language, behavior, and attitude are all motivated to cooperate with the indwelling Spirit. Just as a person who is intoxicated may laugh at things that are not funny and be friendly to people he or she may not like very much, a person *intoxicated* on the Spirit of God will be filled with joy regardless of the circumstances. A Spirit-filled person can love people who don't deserve it and find happiness in circumstances that would otherwise be depressing.

A depressed man went to the doctor to ask for medication. The doctor gave him a prescription, and the man filled it at the local pharmacy. A couple of weeks later, the man came to see the doctor. When the doctor asked if the medication had failed, the patient said, "I don't know what you gave me, but you are going to have to give me something else." When the doctor asked why the patient wanted a different prescription, the man said, "This past week I felt so good that I was speaking to people at church that I don't even like."

I am sure that little story is not true; however, the medicine that can make Christians kind and loving is available through the infilling of the Spirit of God! When God's Spirit fills our lives, He controls how we think, talk, and act. We literally come under the influence of God! Sadly, being filled with the Spirit is one of the most neglected issues in the Christian life today, and as a result, we do not experience or share God's love as we should. Being filled with the Holy Spirit grants believers power, direction, and wisdom that they do not and cannot possess otherwise.

Paul tells us that we must be filled with the Spirit, and then we can speak to each other and sing to the Lord with melody in our hearts. We will learn the language and music of heaven when we are filled with the Spirit of God! Many Christians speak words of bitterness, prejudice, disagreement, and discord simply because they are not filled with the Holy Spirit.

For many senior adult Christians, the infilling of the Holy Spirit can be the single-most important step to finding the assistance needed to deal with the burden of growing old. As we age, our strength is diminished. We can't handle things the way we did when we were young. We can be guilty of concentrating on all the negatives in life. We can become crabby and difficult to deal with. Some older people will say, "Hardly anyone comes around anymore." That may be true because people are simply too busy to do so, and that is likely the case; however, it may be that people aren't comfortable around us because we magnify things that are negative. If you are filled with the Spirit, the presence of Jesus is real to you, and the glow of His presence can be seen by others in your life. People love to be around folks who are upbeat and filled with a positive attitude. When one is filled with the spirit, he or she will speak in *hymns and psalms* from the heart. In other words, you will have words of praise and joy on your lips.

COMPETENCE

Competence. The infilling of God's Spirit makes us competent to serve Him. We may have many natural gifts and abilities and we may also possess many learned abilities or faculties, but to serve God properly, we need the power of the Holy Spirit. Note the passage found in Exodus 28:3: "So you shall speak to all who are gifted artisans, whom I have filled with the spirit of wisdom, that they may make Aaron's garments, to consecrate him, that he may minister to Me as priest."

Note that God was giving instructions on the making of the garments for Aaron so he could properly serve as a priest before God. The Lord spoke to Moses, telling him to speak to the gifted artisans about making the garments. There is no doubt that certain people were gifted with the ability to make fine garments, but when God spoke about them, he told Moses to find those who were filled with the divine spirit of wisdom. There may have been some artisans who were naturally gifted with the ability to make garments, but they were not specifically filled with the divine *spirit* of wisdom. We know that being filled with the Spirit of God is different in the New Testament than it was in the Old Testament, but the important point here is that competence in God's work comes from being gifted by God. In the New Testament, this applies directly to being filled with God's Spirit. I may be able to preach because I have completed degrees of higher education in divinity schools or seminaries, but I will never do the job God wants me to do simply by learning or having natural skills. To do God's work at my best, I must be filled with His Spirit.

Every child of God has the Spirit of God dwelling within. If you don't have the Spirit of God, you do not belong to Him (Romans 8:9). But not every Christian is *filled* with the Spirit. If we were all filled with the Spirit of God, Paul would not have written to the Ephesians instructing us to be *filled.* And in fact, Ephesians 5:18 actually reads *"be always being filled."* In other words, it is something we must continue to consider, otherwise we will simply have the Spirit of God in us, but we will not experience His absolute control over us; and in that case, we do not enjoy the divine competence needed to serve Him effectively. In other words, we must allow the Spirit of God to do in us what He wishes to do so that He can do through us that which He alone can do!

COOPERATION

Cooperation. If we are filled with the Spirit of God, we will be cooperative with others in doing God's work. Notice in Ephesians 5:18 that Paul mentions *submitting* to one another. In other words, where the Spirit of the Lord is ruling and reigning in the hearts of the people, they will cooperate with each other. That is how great things are done in His name. Anyone holding a grudge against another Christian is not filled with the Spirit of God. I'm not saying that a person can live in God's work without getting his or her feelings hurt from time to time; after all, even Jesus was deserted by His disciples. When Jesus prayed with agony in Gethsemane, His disciples slept. He said, "What! Could not watch with me one hour? (Matthew 26:40)." When we are walking in the fullness of the Spirit, we will get our feelings hurt, but that will not slow down our effort to serve God faithfully. Just because the disciples slept while Jesus prayed, Jesus did not throw up His hands and say, "Well, if they are not going to help me, I'm out of here!" I am sure that every Christian has seen people quit because they didn't get their way or because others were not helping with the work or because they weren't getting enough attention for their efforts.

To remain close to Jesus, we need to follow Him, and we need to be filled with the Spirit of God. But there is one more thing required in order to stay close to Christ.

PRAY

In an earlier chapter we dealt with praying correctly, but it is impossible to consider the importance of *focus* in the Christian life without at least a cursory word on the subject of prayer at this point.

If you love someone, you will remain in communication with that person. It is nature of love to be in contact with that which is loved. The senior adult Christian should make it a practice to talk to the Lord faithfully. Keeping a correct Christian focus demands a faithful, active prayer life.

How can we expect to remain close to the Lord if we are not talking to Him? Prayer at its most simplified level is the act of speaking with God. This requires a two-way communication. To pray properly, the child of God must spend some time in God's Word—His love letter—the Bible. God speaks to us through His Word. Then we need to pray with pauses to give God time to speak to us. The clearest leadership I have received from God in my life has come through times of prayer. Often I have found the answer to some issue just after I prayed, while I am praying, and on occasion the answer came long after I prayed. But without prayer, the answer would not have been opened to me.

Prayer can bring leadership from God, peace with God, and power to serve God into our lives. When we pray properly, we align ourselves with God's will. We submit to Him, and He showers us with His love. He opens our eyes so we can see that things are not as bad as we think they are. We see Him in control of situations that beforehand we were trying to handle all alone. Pray! Pray! Pray! Submit before His throne. He will grant you a peace that goes beyond understanding.

To keep our focus right, we must

1. *love Him,*

2. *be filled with His Spirit, and*

3. *pray sincerely.*

We can remain close to Christ, and when we are truly close to Him, we will be faithful in worship, ready to give, bold in our witness, committed to serve, and at peace in our hearts no matter our age or the generation in which we live.

FOCUS APPLICATION

Which king allowed his wives to lead him to worship false gods in the last years of his life? _____.

Name the Bible reference that tells us that the king allowed his wives to lead him to worship false gods?

_____.

_____can lead to ruin since it means we can let down our Guard spiritually.

Solomon's father was _____.

Solomon's father failed God due to his relationship with Bathsheba. Where were the other kings when David stayed home and fell to temptation and sin?

_____.

Since David was a man after God's own heart and Solomon was blessed with God's wisdom, what do their sins tell us about believers and temptation?

_____.

Why was Solomon's sin more dangerous than David's sin?

_____.

King Hezekiah was guilty of what human frailty?

_____.

Arrogance or_____is especially abhorrent to God.

When we are disobedient through pride, selfishness, or laziness, what does He do about it?

_____.

What three things can we do to help ensure that we do not lose our focus on God and His will for our lives?

_____.

CONCLUSION

This study has not included information on diet, exercise, medical issues, and other factors that affect the overall well-being of senior adults. I have not dealt directly with the subject of grief, though that is a subject that senior Christians often face. There are a lot of other books written specifically to address those subjects. My goal has been to enlighten and encourage senior adult Christians in steps that can be taken to brighten their days and increase their effectiveness in serving the Lord. The focus of this book has been to point out some of the most important issues related to the senior Christian's life in and for Christ. If our walk with the Lord is not what it should be, we are going to stumble along and never enjoy the full benefits of having lived into our senior years as believers.

Growing older carries with it blessings and burdens, and sometimes the burdens contain the seeds of our greatest blessings. We must simply trust God in order to see Him bring the burden seed to the full flower of blessing. That doesn't mean that our lives will be easy, and being older can make life even more difficult; however, when one is living for Jesus, there is always a purpose to what he or she is experiencing. Looking for the Lord in all the encounters and incidents we face each day can serve as a means of keeping us from wasting the wonderful advanced years that God has given us. No matter what we are facing, He is with us, will bless us, and will use us as we follow Him faithfully.

As Christians, there are times when we would like to reach out and actually touch the Lord, the way His disciples did. They could literally follow in his human footsteps. For many Christians living in these modern times, it can seem that Jesus is far away. The poet F.W.H. Myers wrote:

> "Oh to have watched thee through the vineyards wander,
> Pluck the ripe ears, and into evening roam!
> Followed, and known that in the twilight yonder
> Legions of angels shone about thy home!"[22]

But, the Lord is with us. He promised that His Spirit would abide with us and in us. As our faith increases, our sense of His presence, power and direction will be more real to us. And, one day, we will see those angels glowing brightly around His home – the home He has prepared for us! Till that day arrives, we are to keep discovering ways to honor Him, love Him and serve Him.

Our senior years bring lots of changes. As Ziggy, the cartoon character once said, "I've finally reached the age when my wild oats have turned into All-Bran![23] But with all the changes occurring as you age, I hope the six steps mentioned in this study have helped you refocus your faith and recommit your life in the service of Christ. Enjoy these years as super years because you have been blessed by the Lord to reach this point in life. W. Somerset Maugham wrote, "Old age has its pleasures, which, though different, are not less than the pleasures of youth."[24] We must not despise God's goodness in granting us the pleasures of old age. Spend time today thanking Him for giving you the gift of advanced years and ask Him to help you enjoy them rather than just asking him to help you endure them.

Frank A. Clark wrote, "We've put more effort into helping folks reach old age than into helping them enjoy it."[25] It is my prayer that this study has and will help you enjoy your senior adult years and that they will be *super years of life* for you.

ENDNOTES

1   Billy Graham, *Newsweek,* August 14, 2006.
2   Senior Journal (www.seniorjournal.com), Available from http://seniorjournal.com/NEWS/ SeniorStats/2011/20111201-SenCitNowLargest. htm, Accessed: 1/7/12.
3   Mickey Mantle, *New York Times,* August 14, 1995, Available from http://topics.nytimes.com/top/ reference/timestopics/people/m/mickey_mantle/ index.html, Accessed: 12/27/11.
4   Available from http://www.brainyquote.com/ quotes/quotes/j/jbpriest383330.html, Accessed: 3/22/12.
5   Traditional lyrics, author unknown.
6   Anon.
7   Tye Tribbett, www.tyetribbettworldwide.com, Accessed 4/11/12.
8   Woody Allen, Available at http://www.imdb.com/ name/nm0000095/bio, Accessed: 2/1/12.

9   Dottie Rambo and Jimmie Davis, Peer Music, Ltd., 1969.

10   Mossie Lister, Words and Music, 1958.

11   Edward Mote, 1836 (Public Domain).

12   Source unknown.

13   Joseph H. Gilmore, 1862 (Public Domain).

14   Available from http://abcnews.go.com/Technology/DyeHard/story?id=460987&page=1#.TwX5_fJyypg Accessed: 4/1/12.

15   Available from http://www.hymnal.net/hymn.php/h/953 Accessed: 2/9/12.

16   James S. Stewart, *The Strong Name* (Grand Rapids, MI: Baker House Books, 1974) pp. 125–167.

17   R. C. Sproul, *Surprised By Suffering: The Role of Pain and Death in the Christian Life* (Wheaton, IL: Tyndale House Publishers, 1998, 2009) p. 1.

18   Randy Alcorn, *If God Is Good: Faith in the Midst of Suffering* (Colorado Springs, CO: Multnomah Books, 2009), p. 22.

19   Lyrics by Charles Albert Tindley.

20   Roy B. Zuck, *The Preacher's Quote Book* (Grand Rapids, MI: Kregel Publications, 2009), p. 363.

21   Source Unknown.

22   Available from http://christianbookshelf.org/meyer/john_the_baptist/iii_his_schools_and_schoolmasters.htm Accessed: 10/3/2012

23   Tom Wilson, *Ziggy*, November 19, 1999.

24   W. Somerset Maugham, *The Summing Up* (New York: The New American Library, 1938) p. 179.

25   Frank A. Clark, *The Country Parson* (Publisher and Date Unknown – book out of print).